Praise for
Resilient War

"…Benas and Buzz continue to understand and execute on their why, and they have enlisted the help of their friends to provide a lead by example guide on resiliency."
— **Daniel Rodriguez,** U.S. Army veteran & actor

"I am a huge believer of being creative and adaptive in any situation. In addition, I feel how you do one thing is how you do everything. What separates greatness from normality are people who can withstand what others can't".
— **Steve Hess,** longtime Denver Nuggets Strength & Conditioning Coach

"*The Resilient Warrior* is the ultimate guide to creating a life of peace, happiness and contentment, not just for veterans trying to readjust to civilian life, but for anyone who wants to live life on their terms."
— **Lee-Anne Gilchrist,** performance coach & motivational speaker

"Incredibly important focus, the subject is universally relatable."
— **Chris Canestrari,** Sales Leader/Coach

"This book is the red dawn for one's soul."
— **Paul Guarino,** founder of PG Sports

"The knowledge compiled by the authors in this book is invaluable!"

—**Joe Wadanoli,** master barber & Auxiliary
Coast Guard Service Member

"*The Resilient Warrior* is a book that provides an easy reference to find the help you need, when you need it most. Nick Benas has provided the literary and self-help world with access to best practice strategies for individuals experiencing difficult life moments."

—**Michele Hart,** LCSW, author of *Mental Health Emergencies*

"As an Army Nurse who served in Iraq 2003–2004, reintegration after combat is a continuous process that last through the service-member's life. *The Resilient Warrior* brings much needed insight for all who have served to be able to overcome, adapt and cope with the rigors of serving. Well-written, touches home, highly recommend this to anyone who has served or is serving!"

—**Jessica M. Diaz,** US Army Nurse Corps

"Buzz Bryan and Nick Benas masterfully do it again—doling out compelling self-help tactics that are not just for the 1% of us who served in America's wars, but for all of us who want to better ourselves and our families."

—**Patrick J. Murphy,** 32nd Under Secretary of the
Army & America's First Iraq Veteran in Congress

THE
RESILIENT
WARRIOR

Battle-Tested Life Hacks
for Military Men & Women

Nick Benas &
Buzz Brian

Hatherleigh Press is committed to preserving and protecting
the natural resources of the earth. Environmentally
responsible and sustainable practices are embraced
within the company's mission statement.

Visit us at www.hatherleighpress.com and register online
for free offers, discounts, special events, and more.

THE RESILIENT WARRIOR

Library of Congress Cataloging-in-Publication Data is available.

ISBN: 978-1-57826-920-4

Printed in the United States

10 9 8 7 6 5 4 3 2 1

*To Gunnery Sergeant John Basilone, United States
Marine Corps*
Medal of Honor & Navy Cross
4 November 1916 to 19 February 1945

Contents

PART I:
TACTICS FOR EMOTIONAL HEALTH

PART II:
TACTICS FOR SELF-CARE

PART III:
TACTICS FOR MIND/BODY SUPPORT

Authors' Note

O
N THE OUTSKIRTS of Pittsburgh, tucked away in rural suburbia, two government sedans rolled down a long and winding gravel driveway. Road pebbles hitting the wheel wells, the cars pulled up to a modest raised ranch home. Buzz and his colleague Bill, Transition Patient Advocates with the VA, parked in front of the wrap-around porch and confirmed the address. Both men exited their vehicles, well-presenting in their neatly pressed slacks, crisp shirts, and ties.

They stepped onto the porch and knocked on the front door. Nothing.

They knocked again. No answer.

Buzz glanced around the porch and pointed out to Bill what appeared to be a deliberate arrangement of garlic cloves, squirrel tails and raccoon tails, along with a silver bucket filled with corn and dried corn cobs. The pungent smell of garlic in the air was apparent.

Buzz and Bill walked around the premises. They noted a downstairs bedroom window open, and sensed someone was home. They headed back to the porch, knocked again and the vet slowly made his appearance at the door. The former combat veteran, an Army MP who had served in Iraq, had gone from being engaged in PTSD treatment through the VA to isolating himself and off meds. Buzz and Bill, himself a retired Army colonel, were sent to check on him.

Buzz asked to come in, the vet agreed, and the three men sat down at a long wooden table—Buzz and Bill at one end, the combat vet at the other. Buzz opened the conversation.

"We're here just to get eyeballs on you. The clinical staff are concerned because you haven't been showing up for your appointments; they have not been able to contact you and we wanted to know how you're doing," he began. "We also want to know if there are any barriers you are experiencing with the VA and to let you know you can contact us at any time so that we can help you. We're not here to take you anywhere or say you have to do this or that; we just want to make sure you're OK and all is good."

For 10 to 15 minutes, each man recounted stories of his own service. Tensions eased, and the vet rose from the table and said he had something he needed to put away. Buzz and Bill observed at this point the vet was holding a .38 revolver in his hand, and it dawned on them he had had it under the table—aimed directly at them from the time they sat down.

"I'm sorry about this," the vet explained. "I knew I had to carry this because there was no way I was going anywhere with you today."

After some nervous laughter and crude commentary, Buzz (having already noted the exits of the residence), said, "Listen, if you're going to shoot, shoot him first," pointing to Bill. "He's older; I'm faster, and I can get out of here!"

As Buzz and Bill were leaving, Buzz said, "Listen, I grew up in the city, I don't know much about this stuff, so I have to ask you something."

"Sure thing," the vet replied, taking a drag on his cigarette.

"I noticed outside on your porch—there's these squirrel tails and metal buckets…what's it for?'

The man's eyes lit up, and he said, "I'll tell you; the squirrel tails keep me safe from the demons and creatures of the night. The garlic keeps vampires away. And the silver bucket's for the werewolves."

Buzz, an advocate for Veteran's Health Services, would meet these individuals where they were. Often, Buzz and his team would receive phone calls from the crisis hotline or social workers within the Veteran's Health Administration asking for assistance with veterans. Buzz and colleagues would go out in the field and check up on these fellow warriors; they'd search under bridges, stop by local jails, visit homes and hospital emergency rooms.

This life experience is the catalyst for this book.

It affected Buzz to know a dude was willing to shoot him before he would go back to treatment. You never know what you are walking into, the circumstances, why they are feeling the way they are, what's going on in their lives, or what some clerk at the VA said to them when they may or may not have reached out for help/assistance.

Foreword

by Kortney Yasenka, LCMHC

A S A LICENSED clinician mental health counselor, I see firsthand the struggle that many endure when it comes to living your best life. This can be especially true for veterans and active-duty personnel. The life of a warrior can be both rewarding and exhausting physically and mentally speaking. The very virtues that make warriors strong, resilient, determined, and persistent, on the battlefield can often cause the opposite effect off the battlefield. Many veterans' brains have an extremely difficult time adjusting once active duty is over and civilian life resumes. This is one of the main reasons I have such high regard for *The Resilient Warrior*. The authors, Benas and Buzz, have done a tremendous job identifying areas of need and pairing those with warriors who are doing the self-care themselves and providing the invaluable tips/strategies that may help those struggling veterans conquer and defeat their personal obstacles in order to succeed on the battlefield of life.

During my years as a therapist, I have worked with a variety of individuals who suffer from different mental illnesses, but none have been more fascinating than those who have served in the military. The way in which their brains have been trained no doubt has prepared them to be successful military members. But where has it left them after their tour is over? Where has it left them when they are back home and living the civilian life with friends and family?

It is my great honor to have been asked to participate in this book, *The Resilient Warrior*. These two authors have done a tremendous job bringing awareness and a sense of understanding to the veteran and active-duty community. Their willingness to be open and honest with their struggles is both endearing and empowering. We can no longer turn a blind eye to what these warriors have gone through, are going through, and will go through in the future. It is my hope that all who read this book will be equipped with useful, functional, life hacks/tips/strategies to help defeat inner enemies and live a healthier and happier life.

Research indicates there is a high percentage of veterans experiencing mental health issues daily. What can be done to help combat their struggles? Thankfully, these authors and their contributors have been courageously candid with their experiences both positive and negative and share with the readers life hacks to help each warrior live their best possible life.

Given my experience and work with the military community, I have come to find that each warrior has their own unique story, but the same struggles once active duty has come to an end. It's these struggles that make a resource and book like *The Resilient Warrior* so valuable to not only service members but also their friends, family and loved ones.

Warriors, by definition and nature, are fighters. Much of what makes a warrior great is the ability to train his/her brain to be calm and collected during a stressful situation. So, what exactly happens in our brains and bodies when you are faced with a stressful situation?

When faced with a threat, the amygdala, a tiny part of your brain responsible for emotions, is alerted and automatically signals what scientists call the "fight, flight, or freeze" response. This response allows you to prepare your body to either fight, take flight, or freeze. During this time, another part of our brain, the frontal lobe, is trying to determine if danger is indeed actually present and what may be the most appropriate and logical way to respond. However, if the threat or stress is that strong, the amygdala may overpower the frontal lobe and "act without thinking" so to speak.

The amygdala and your brain's stress response are trying to help you. The job of the amygdala is to sense fear and react without hesitation. A situation which veterans are all too familiar with. During times of combat, active warriors must make split second decisions, many not based on long thought-out decisions, but based on instinct. Their brains are trained to automatically respond to a threat as it is often a life-or-death decision. It is all or nothing thinking. There is no middle ground or room for interpretation or different perspectives. The ability to think through a situation is not a luxury that active military personnel are afforded. They rely on their training to make the best decisions and to, quite frankly, keep them and others alive.

While the warriors' training is extremely beneficial during active duty and on the battlefield, let us see how it may play out once they hang up their uniforms.

The brain's ability to be trained and conditioned is possibly at the same time its biggest strength and greatest weakness. Even though you have left active service, does not mean you have easily forgotten your training. Imagine getting ready for bed at night. You put on a pair of comfortable pajamas, get into your soft, cozy bed, and lay down next to a loved one, all while feeling calm and safe. Your body is relaxed and there is nothing on your brain that seems out of the ordinary. You begin to feel tired, and you slowly drift off to sleep.

This situation seems like a typical night for most people. The difference is that when this warrior awakes in the morning, his hands are positioned as if he is holding a gun. Why do you ask? He is not on active duty anymore. In fact, he has been home for years. He is sleeping in his own bed with his family around him in a nice neighborhood. Doesn't he know he is not in any danger anymore?

Unfortunately, just because he is in a different environment physically, his brain is stuck in the past. Even when you are not consciously aware your brain is always on high alert. This is the reason why you may be so easily triggered by loud noises, a dog barking, or even a car horn beeping. Your brain interprets these as threats which cause your body to respond in a fight, flight, or freeze response. You may even start to experience physical symptoms of the stress response, such as an increased heartbeat, rapid breathing, sweaty palms, and possible visual flashbacks. Your body may be walking your dog, but your brain is back in full combat mode.

Your warrior brain is still programmed to view every situation as a possible threat. Remember, this training is the exact way you want your brain to react while on active duty. Every sudden noise or move has the potential to cause harm and your automatic response to prepare for battle is the goal of a warrior. But how do you tell your brain that you are no longer in danger…that the noise you hear is just your dog barking? The tips and strategies to do so are the exact ones laid out in this book. (Insert Book Title) is the first step in retraining your brain in order to live the version of your warrior self on the ever-changing battlefield of life.

When military personnel begin to live a civilian life, their brains are often still stuck in combat mode…figuratively and literally. Science has shown that the amygdala of returning military members is overactive causing greater sensitivity to perceived threats. As you can imagine this can make everyday living and daily activities significantly more difficult. Therefore, it is vital that warriors learn these strategies/hacks while fighting on the battlefield of life. Veterans must develop a new game plan and be given new marching orders for their brain.

This book gives each individual warrior the opportunity to learn new ways of living. You cannot change your past, but what you do in the present can change your future. Everyone, military or not, fights an inner battle every day and everyone, military or not, is a warrior and can win their internal struggle.

Everyone regardless of their past could live a better, healthier, and happier life, which is free of trauma, stress, and unwarranted triggers. It is important as a warrior that you find which life hacks/strategies are most effective and beneficial for you. Everyone is different and everyone copes and handles situations in different ways. One of the many great things about this book is that it does not offer just one life strategy or one game plan. The authors have done a wonderful job at comprising a list of specialists who add different perspectives to the healing model. Coping with life's everyday stressors is not one size fits all. I would encourage all who are reading this book to take an active role in your new marching orders to a better life. Become an active participant in your healing process and do not be afraid to try new things. Increase the size of your comfort zone and open your mind to new perspectives. You now can forge your own path and take control of your own future battles. Remember, warriors are not created alone, rely on Benas and Buzz, your support systems, and this book to help you conquer your inner struggles and be more in control of your future missions.

—Kortney Yasenka, LCMHC

Introduction

"Knowledge, know the ledge to where your heart is or fall off into the internal hell that's uncharted."
—WU TANG CLAN

THE TWO OF us are frequently reminded of signage we once saw splayed on a blast wall back in Iraq: COMPLACENCY KILLS.

That graffiti was our reminder to keep moving, questioning, examining, re-examining, and attacking. It remains our decision to this day to keep moving by adapting and overcoming, skipping the ailments, and the reactionary. Yet many of our fellow warriors are torn and in tatters, empty shells of their former physically and mentally fit selves. Both veterans and those actively serving are stuck, suffering, and often suicidal. Some wage a war within as high-stakes as the war without, and still lose the battle. We are burdened by this truth.

The following pages are our personal exploration of what lies beyond the "traditional methods" of care. We have enlisted the help of our close friends and friends of friends; veterans, divorcees, single mothers of military families, military sexual assault victims, drug and alcohol users, former and active U.S. Marines, Navy, Army, Rangers, Berets, a former member of The British Royals, an auxiliary Coast Guard Member & Master Barber, providers, and caretakers who are practitioners in their respective niche(s).

They are doing the daily rinse and repeat. They are getting themselves unstuck, seeking and practicing with positive, healthy alternatives, all in the name of chipping away and coping with setbacks and struggles. The WARRIORS featured in this book are relentless. They take care of business.

The two of us have made a career out of working and supporting veterans post-military, and we avow that the warrior contributors featured are appropriate for this project. They have expressed comfort in their sharing. They have fostered an aesthetic of smoothness and speed in their operational environments. They continue to shock the enemy, even while others dwindle away their time with the manufactured suffering.

Throughout this book you will hear many voices, each with their own tips and tricks to gaining the upper hand against the powerful enemies of the modern day-to-day. The gains they have won are immeasurable, and now they are offered to you freely.

This book is a field manual for feeling well.

For the Warriors

For those with military backgrounds, we know you have been trained to execute effectively during the toughest of times. You were mentally fit, physically ripped. Know that regaining and managing your physical, mental, and emotional health is possible, with some effort and a desire to change. All warriors deserve to be at peace and free of chaos outside the theatre of war. You need a field manual that works. To lift the fog, you must be motivated. Passivity prevents you from moving forward. Waiting for others to aid and assist will always keep you waiting. You can endure if you want better for yourself and others. Don't get left behind in the reception area of your medical office or the isolation of your home. You alone control your course of action.

And with that, we welcome you WARRIORS. We are honored you are joining the Resilient Warrior community. We thank you for following our writing and exploration. The support we have received after writing *The Warrior's Book of Virtues* has been incredible. The many readers we touched were unexpected, and they inspired us in return. This writing process has motivated us to continue on the path leading to discovery and life-long learning.

We thank you for your commitment to grow and improve, for leveling up and ending suffering. Our hope is that you will lead others on your path to ascension and victory. Your resolve is inspiring.

The Resilient Warrior will...

- Challenge the belief that traditional healthcare has your immediate solution
- Prevent you from becoming a "cog" in a medical treatment plan or healthcare system
- Challenge the belief that medication is the only way out
- Teach you what other WARRIORS are doing for remedy and happiness
- Chip away at the anxiety, depression, and suffering
- Help you regain your confidence and eradicate fears

How to Read This Book

The Resilient Warrior is a collection of easy strategies, practical tips, and self-care ideas for military men and women, and everyday people. Our book is not a solution but an embarkation. You will find hacks that pry the warrior out of isolation.

Hacks are annotated in the table of contents and a list of the Warrior Resources can be found at the back of the book.

We are not doctors, and the following is not a prescription. Do not be stupid, and do not hold us, the contributors featured within, or the publisher accountable. Make sure you proceed with caution. Let the following content be an introduction to novelty, a return to our days of play. This book is an attempt to create more awareness, positive action(s) and a focus on what matters, making you and all of us a more balanced Warrior. We are all in this together, Coalition Forces, Army, Air Force, Coast Guard, National Guard, Reserves, Navy, Marine Corps, friends, and family. Everything you need to help you attack the day is right here. Collaborating on this book has helped us grow in so many ways. We had no idea of the immediate impact this project would have. A big thank you for the warriors that fill the following pages...we are grateful for this newly found friendship and your contributions to help our fellow WARRIORS.

Take the stuff you enjoy from here, do more of it, and do it consistently. Be good to yourself. Make this manual a part of your battle kit and refer to it often. You will have the ability to maximize your healthy habits while adding new life hacks. Taoist philosophy believes that life is always flowing and transforming, and things that are static become dead. Be fluid. WARRIORS keep moving and stun their opponents with great fury.

—Nick Benas USMC & Buzz Bryan USN

"The reason the universe is eternal is that it does not live for itself; it gives life to others as it transforms."
    —Lao Tzu

PART I

TACTICS FOR EMOTIONAL HEALTH

A COMMON JOKE GROWING up in elementary school was: "What did the librarian say to the school children?" Answer? "If you want to hide something, put it in a book."

This would always elicit a few chuckles and make the recipient think about being FOMOKED (Fear Of Missing Out on Knowledge and Education), but in these times it has an even starker meaning. Reality tells us that fewer adults are reading books. Every few years, the National Center for Education Statistics puts out data on adult literacy rates in America, and the results are disquieting.

With this knowledge, we know fewer books are getting read, which is sad, but we also know this is a great opportunity for us to hide some great wisdom within. We are dedicated to the men and women in the military community, and nowhere will you find such a comprehensive field manual for self-care, and wellness. *The Resilient Warrior* is a complete compendium with easy step-by-step instructions. The warriors within the following pages have provided you with the how and the why.

The purpose of *The Resilient Warrior* is to describe an alternative approach to the traditional methods of healthcare that we are all used to, and those long, exhausting, and arduous modalities of treatment providers put us through. This is not meant to be the be-all-end-all, nor are we telling you to discredit any great, sound medical advice and care you have received; we simply want this to be a complement to any existing regimen you may have.

Warrior Wellness is an alternative approach that supports your overall health and well-being. Benas and Buzz have adopted a lifestyle of self-experimentation to continue improving upon, a doctrine that had been instilled in them from Benas' childhood in that small town of Guilford, Connecticut to Buzz's upbringing in the big city of Philadelphia. This desire for self-care was a continuation and became an expectation of their Marine Corps and Navy service. The desire for self-care and wellness for the authors has been a process of reset and reconciliation post military service. They have done the reconnaissance and they have enlisted the help of their close friends, the fellow warriors who are doing incredible things in the name of wellness. The doctrine the authors' have adopted is one that questions and challenges traditional assumptions, and one that evaluates the utility of these strategies to become more healthy, effective, self-satisfied, and able to execute when called upon as WARRIOR.

Lastly, you will be able to increase your physical and mental well-being by assessing your current surroundings, just like you did in regular training in garrison or on deployment in the theatre of combat. Ever present is the sometimes enemy, sometimes friend named stress who, when not controlled or looked after, becomes mounting and chaotic. Stress attacks your whole environment, and is the precursor to many ailments and diseases. When stress takes a grip, it strips your body of good physical and mental health and it wreaks absolute havoc on your mind and body. Stress can be relied on in its earliest stages as a great tactic for your self-awareness and be an alarm for personal safety. Learn to pay attention to stress and it will guide you in your battles of everyday living. Learn to pay attention to the signs and symptoms; it will come by way of physical manifestations, and often it will display with certain behaviors, and it will take hold physically with depleted energy, migraines/headaches, tension throughout the body (body/muscle aches, pains, constipation, diarrhea, nausea).

Our holistic approach is meant as one more tactic for our brothers and sisters. It is not a remedy or a prescription, but it *is* a start for those who may be starting to slip or are becoming a victim of complacency. We have a duty to our brothers and sisters; and we have a duty to pick each other up. We see you. The suffering may not be visible to those on the outside, but we understand there is great pain, difficulty, and suffering. The pain may be emotional or physical, a combination of both, and there feels like no escape.

This subject matter is a tough one; we all have our different experiences, just like the complexities of war, no one is really equipped or prepared to talk about it or live with it. For most of us there may have been a moment in time when our mental and physical health was performing at an optimal level and now the vanity is slipping. The many tactics found in the following pages will expose you to some remarkably simple things that you can do to start to get better. From hygiene to hobby, from bubble baths to breathing, we will provide you with a fully comprehensive self-help guide to living a healthy, fulfilled, and better life—the WARRIOR way.

Just like the old Marine Corps recruiting poster says: *"We don't promise you a rose garden."* But we, as band of brothers and sisters, need to be a force in wellness. We need to share the following content far and wide. Open the book and proceed.

Keep the Best and Leave the Rest

Vanessa Jacoby, PhD, ABPP
Advisor with Clarity Child Guidance Center

Evaluate the situation and create a lifestyle strategy that best fits your circumstances, utilizing what works and removing what doesn't.

For many, being a military service member is not just a job. Military service is surrounded by unique culture, values, and lifestyle. Some service members embrace their military culture and training and bring those values home to their families. Others try to intentionally separate themselves from the "soldier" at work and the "parent and spouse" at home.

There is no specific "right" way to do things and different strategies work for different families. However, in working with military families, I have noticed that the families who are struggling tend to take an extreme approach at either end of this spectrum—the "All or None" approach.

Most things in life are not black and white. "All or nothing" thinking is a common yet unhelpful thinking pattern that can cause problems in our lives. This is true for bringing your military training and values into your home, as well. On the one hand, many military values may have great benefits and are meant to create strong and resilient people. Who doesn't want their family to be strong and resilient?

Likewise, completely isolating your family from military life can lead your family to feel left out on top of missing out on the unique strengths that come with being in a military family. On the other hand, the military has a specific purpose, and they train people to behave in order to fulfill that purpose. That means that not all aspects of military training and values, rigidly followed, make sense in the context of raising children.

Here are key military values that are great to bring into the family (with moderation) plus a couple of additional values that are essential to good child development.

The Hack Unpacked

So, what to keep, and what to toss?

High expectations. The military famously "breaks you down to build you back up." They test your limits, push you to the max. They need you to be not just good, but great. This is because service members often encounter life-threatening situations, and a service member being unskilled could have life or death consequences for themselves or others. It is the nature of the job.

When it comes to our family, it is important to consider the difference in context between training for a warzone and parenting. Setting high expectations communicates to your children that you believe in them and that they can accomplish great things. However, it is especially important that the expectations placed upon them are *developmentally and individually appropriate.* Consider your children's age, as well as their unique strengths and struggles while keeping in mind that no one can be great at everything. When you set expectations unrealistically high, you are setting your child up for failure which could have negative consequences on their self-esteem.

Teamwork. The military is composed of many teams. Missions can only be successfully completed through effective teamwork. Teamwork means that each person on a team (or in a family) is important and makes meaningful contributions. When one member of the team is successful, we all celebrate that success. When one member of the team is struggling, we rally around to support them. Teaching children to work together as a team can set them up for success in school, with peers, and in adulthood. Building teamwork in families works best when parents can balance this value with also spending time and showing affection for each of their children individually.

Give it your all. Military training teaches you that when you set out to accomplish a goal, you give it your all—you do not do things halfway. In a military mission, a service member may go as far as injuring themselves to complete the mission for the sake of the team. This goes back to teamwork—each member of the team is important. On military missions, one person not completing a task can have dire consequences for others.

Like high expectations, it is important to keep the *context* of the environment in mind when teaching perseverance to your children. There is an important difference between completing a task at war and, for example, not dropping an AP class or finishing a soccer game. Teaching integrity can help a child build self-esteem and strength as they accomplish difficult goals and are praised for "putting in their all." Yet, when it comes to children's developing minds and bodies, it is important to recognize that it is possible to push a child too hard, leading to injury (for a physical task) and unhelpful, distressing anxiety or self-criticism.

Vigilance. It's common military saying: "Stay alert, stay alive." In combat, vigilance is essential. Service members live in extremely dangerous environments in which an enemy is out to harm them.

There are, of course, dangers that children should be aware of. Traffic, bullies and even child predators. However, when teaching children to be vigilant, it is important to use *developmentally appropriate* language. Three-year-olds and thirteen-year-olds understand the concept of danger very differently, and conversations around safety should reflect that. Also, remember that difference in *context*. While dangers clearly exist in this world, our children are not fighting an enemy and so the dangers are less probable. When discussing safety with your children, be sure to differentiate between "situational awareness" and hypervigilance or paranoia. While the first can help our children stay safe, the second can lead to phobias, chronic worry, and anxiety.

Self-Control. In the military, self-control and inner strength are essential, and are often represented by training service members to maintain a sense of stoicism. While strength and self-control are wonderful values to teach our children, the best *way* to teach children is not the same as how it is trained in service members. To understand this, it is important to consider *children's development* and *context* in which stoicism is used. In war, you are expected to see and experience incredibly difficult and even traumatic events. There may be times that you must push through them or "drink water, drive on" to survive.

In contrast, our goal in raising children is to provide a nurturing, safe, and predictable environment. Therefore, the context of the environment is completely different than at war. In fact, when raising children, it is our job as parents to teach our children to identify and appropriately express our full range of emotions. This means teaching our children to *regulate* the expression of emotions (which is where self-control comes in), but not to ignore or hide them.

And what should you add?

Military training and values have the potential to provide so much for service members and their families. And yet, because of the *context* and purpose of the military, they cannot provide all that is needed to raise children. Below are a few things to consider intentionally adding to your parenting toolbox. I want to stress here that the principles below are in no way incongruent with military culture. In fact, I would argue that they fit right in and many service members who are successful and satisfied in their jobs use these tools.

Two-way communication. For important reasons, the military is structured in strict hierarchies. While there are individual differences in leadership styles, much information is communicated in one direction, on a "need to know" basis, and service members can be punished for questioning leadership authority. Hierarchy is important in families as well. Parents are largely the decision makers and children should not be given *all* of the information all of the time. Yet, as our children develop, so should our communication with them.

Giving children developmentally appropriate information and allowing them opportunities to provide input about family experiences, transitions, and decisions is essential for children to make meaning of and experience some sense of control in the world. In contrast, keeping children in the dark because "they are just children" can be frustrating, confusing, and scary.

Emotional connection. You can think of this as the flip side of stoicism. Our children need to know that we are there for them not only physically, but also emotionally. This means providing an environment that makes it safe to appropriately express any emotions (by appropriately, I mean saying "I'm angry" vs. hitting your sister), and that you appropriately share your emotions with the family as well. This doesn't mean sharing all emotions you have all the time. However, it does mean sharing enough that your family can understand your actions. This emotional connection is vital for your children to build a strong and healthy attachment to you and your spouse.

Finding your balance. All families are unique. What works for one family may not work for another, and it may take some trial and error to find the right balance of how much to incorporate (or not) military values into your family. If you work to keep in mind the *context* and intention of these values, as well as how to incorporate them in *developmentally appropriate* ways for your children, be confident. That balance will come.

Practicing Parental Support

Joshua Essery, PsyD, ABPP
Director of Outpatient Clinical Services
at Clarity Child Guidance Center

Ensure that your routines integrate physical activity, a healthy diet, regular fun, time in nature, ongoing supportive relationships, and connection with the community.

"Diane" is the adoptive mother of three girls who experienced severe trauma as toddlers and suffered serious emotional and behavioral disorders as a result. After months of treatment and care, her pre-teens are doing well, but Diane is vigilant about keeping them safe and healthy.

She writes: "Exercise, as we know, is great for not only physical health, but also for mental and family health, too. We have adopted the practice of going on nature hikes, fishing, bike riding and even entering some 5ks to bring physical health and family time together. Aside from the obvious benefits, sometimes, when the kids are out of the natural environment (school and home), they tend to open up more about the things on their mind. And without the distractions of electronics and such, they can 'hear' us better and also process their own thoughts and feelings more easily."

Habits and life routines affect our mental health and well-being. So, what can military and veteran parents do to create a better mental health for our children?

Being aware of mental health is an important part of caring for ourselves and our children. In a seminal article titled "Lifestyle and Mental Health," Roger Walsh, PhD, professor at the University of California Irving College of Medicine, presents research that identifies multiple lifestyle factors to support overall mental health. The following is a list of important lifestyle variables that affect mental health with some related questions to reflect on:

Physical activity. Are there regular times for exercise built into your schedule? How often do you or your child engage in activities that require physical effort? Do you have a list of local programs that can help your child stay active?

Time in nature. Do you and your family members spend time in natural sunlight, away from screens and electronics? Are there regular opportunities to get fresh air in a natural setting such as a park or forest preserve? Explore the fun with the help of your local Parks and Recreation Department.

Diet. Does your family have a routine where family members are eating a balanced diet? Are the number of calories you or your children consume balanced with what is needed given your physical output and body type? How much sugar, caffeine, artificial or processed foods do you or your child consume?

Sleep. How many hours of restful sleep do you or your children get per night? Do you and your children have a regular and stable sleep routine that supports true rest?

Fun. How and in what ways do you and your children play? Are there regular times where laughter, excitement, and enjoyable experiences take place? If not, why not and how might you alter your routines and activities to make time for carefree fun and play?

Relationships. Do you and your family members engage in supportive relationships that are defined by trust and openness while maintaining appropriate boundaries? Do you and your children regularly spend time with friends in person? Does your family have an adequate support system?

Community/spiritual involvement. How often does your family attend community-related events or spiritually oriented activities? Are there times when your family engages in activities that contribute to the larger good of your community and serve others? Do you and your children feel a connection with the larger community and have a greater sense of meaning and purpose?

You may choose to take an assessment of how your family is supporting mental health through therapeutic lifestyle choices. Make it a priority to ensure that your routines integrate physical activity, a healthy diet, regular fun, time in nature, ongoing supportive relationships, and connection with the community. While identifying mental health conditions and symptoms is essential, making therapeutic lifestyle choices can improve our quality of life while helping prevent mental health problems for us and our children. For more information about good mental health, check claritycgc.org or go to claritycgc.org/military for military-specific issues.

Outside Your Comfort Zone

Nathan John
British Army, Royal Signals

Step outside your comfort zone in order to escape life's struggles, remove barriers and experience new healthy gains.

When you are out of your comfort zone, take a moment to pause for thought.

In the military, we are trained to operate under the most testing of circumstances—and for good reason: anyone who has served in the US or British Army at some point in the last 20 years were highly likely to have found themselves on operations in the Middle East, a hostile environment with an invisible enemy. This is highly stressful.

Having left the Army in 2018, I have had time to reflect on the lessons that have had the biggest impact on my life, those lessons that truly shape one's character. I cannot speak to everyone's experiences, but for me I always found the subtleties the most life-changing. Yes, the highly charged environment of an advance to contact on a training exercise was exhilarating; smoke, the crack of small arms fire and (if you were lucky) some high explosive battlefield simulator explosions, too. These experiences gave me a short-term adrenaline boost, one which I've found still enables me to raise my game when the going gets tough in my life after service.

But I have to say, those experiences have been few and far between. What I have found most useful is the training where soldiers and officers are taught to control their emotions. This was introduced subtly and over time. As a soldier, there were times every year when we would go on adventure training. And while it may have looked like a holiday from an outsider's perspective (and quite possibly from some on the inside, too), the rationale for sending soldiers sports parachuting, diving in the Red Sea, canoeing in the USA, mountaineering in Nepal, among almost every other conceivable extreme sport, was to take that person and put them in a situation that they weren't used to—outside their comfort zone, so to speak. And so I have sat, afraid, on the edge of an open door of an aeroplane preparing to take a leap of faith, asking myself whether I'd packed my parachute properly, and what if it doesn't open, what if the reserve fails, what if I don't jump, everybody's looking at me…

In those few seconds spent outside of our comfort zones, you are under extreme stress—and you are fighting with every fiber in your body to take back control.

Militarily, in planning for operations sleep deprivation is a common tool used in the US and British Armies as a foundation in training in the field. This again is to take you outside of your routine of rising in the morning, having a leisurely breakfast, going to work doing a bit of PT and finally going home or back to the barrack block at the end of the day. Our experiences on operations have taught us that there is no schedule in conflict, so we must be prepared 24 hours per day to operate effectively. We do this for years whether you have served 1 year or 30 years, but then it stops! We leave and go into the civilian workplace, once again you are outside of your comfort zone.

It took me two years to figure out that I was the one who wasn't normal. I do not mean that in a negative way, mind you;

what I mean is, I had been trained to do certain things—but more importantly than that, I had an ingrained set of values and standards that I would always strive to meet. To my almost daily surprise, I discovered that the people I worked with had a different motivation and work ethic to me. This challenged me in ways I'd never been challenged before; I had always led soldiers and been good at it, so what had changed?

The simple answer is civilians are not soldiers. They usually are not highly trained or constantly developed to do a job; rather, they go to work, do their job, and go home as soon as it's time to punch out. After the first 12 months in my new life as a civilian, I became demotivated and frustrated. I reminisced about my time in the military and longed for that same team spirit I had previously enjoyed. When I asked for something to be done, I would be told it was done, and normally (that is, in the military) I could believe that to be true—because it was true. Not so in civilian life; I soon realised that integrity was in short supply and teamwork was a scarcity that I'd taken for granted for decades.

Frustrated to a point of despair almost daily, I needed to find a strategy that would work for me. My mental health was at stake, so I thought back to the first principles I had learned during my time in training. Guns or bayonet range training probably would not help me here, but what I could think back to was how, when I was under the most stress, with pressure coming from all sides including my superior officer, my own soldiers and my peers needing me to do something, I'd adjusted to the strain.

When stress and anxiety start to consume me, I often go to a café and have a coffee alone. If that is not available, then I will go for a walk and forget everything. The knot in my chest starts to unwind and my heartbeat eases back to something more normal. This is my own form of self-medication, my solution for when the world starts to close in. The pause for thought helped me jump out of that aircraft, it helped me work for 48 hours without sleep, it helped me support my team under fire in Iraq and helped me keep my head on patrols in Afghanistan.

Life for veterans is both a gift and a curse. We are the luckiest people on the planet: we are able to forge the strongest relationships, connect with a like-minded community across the world and have instantaneous trust by knowing that the person you're speaking with has also served. The other edge to this sword is our struggles in assimilating into and understanding a life out of uniform, with its irrational complexity and selfishness. But! We are a community of WARRIORS. There is and always will be a serviceperson or veteran who will help; all we need do is ask for it. And before that, pause for thought.

In uniform and out of uniform, the single most effective hack I have used to get me through difficult situations is to pause for thought, to reflect on the strategy of the situation, the bigger picture, because it is highly likely that it is the tactics that are causing the stress. It can be a few seconds or a few hours, it is less about time and more about you. When you are out of your comfort zone, pause for thought.

Anger Management

Rev. Bernice Sykes, Ph.D. "Doc Bunny"
United States Army

Identify, recognize, and manage anger and certain behaviors.

I am a veteran who lives with Post Traumatic Stress Disorder (PTSD). There were times when PTSD managed me instead of the other way around; times when I did not have information about how to effectively deal with life and with the symptoms I was experiencing daily. At that time, I felt lost and without hope. One day, I decided the time of me being helpless was over, and I needed to find a battle plan for accomplishing this task.

If there was one thing that helped me understand PTSD, it would be understanding my anger. When people refer to anger, they treat it like the enemy. Yet the approach that helped me most was making my anger my best friend, by embracing it. In understanding your anger like it is your best friend, it ceases to be scary.

Since anger is almost always a component in any issue related to mental health, we are taught to repress and/or suppress those feelings when something is bothering us. In the Army, for example, when you are ordered to do something questionable, you learn to "suck it up". Anger also rears its ugly head when you are going through the transition of leaving service, whether at the end of your contract or during retirement. Anger always seems to be present when receiving a medical diagnosis or personal news that requires you to make sudden changes to your lifestyle, forcing you to make adjustments you normally would not have. As a veteran or a retiree, our skills for coping with anger are something that we need to work on and develop to live our best lives after serving our country.

Coming to terms with my anger meant taking my symptoms seriously and being committed to making necessary changes in my perspective when it comes to controlling anger. It meant no more saying that everything is fine when it is not. It meant my guiding purpose in finding happiness in life was planning ways to greatly reduce the role anger played and executing that plan.

To make a plan, first you need information. What I am about to discuss is accomplished best when working with a mental health professional. With a few exceptions, most veterans can receive that help at Veteran Administration Centers (VA Centers). But before you take that to mean your counselor is going to do all your work for you, think again. We must participate in our own recovery which means doing the work. However, if you want to work an issue out on your own and get some assistance when you think you need it, that is fine. Just remember to delegate if it gets to be too much. What helped me most were the following three tools I used when taking my anger management classes:

Identify your triggers. Anger is fear. Probably one of the most important skills that is important in reducing anger is learning to identify situations that bring fear and understanding how *you* are reacting to what is taking place. The issue is not always what someone else did, it also comes with the emotions of how someone made you feel. If you are continuously being disrespected at work, you may take serious offense to a simple misunderstanding by someone who has nothing to do with the hostile environment and damage an otherwise good relationship because you are afraid to confront the larger issue of workplace bullying. I had to learn to use a number scale to track my anger. I know it takes a while for me to get to a 6 on my trigger meter, but I also know that once I am a 6, it does not take much more to get me to 10. I am going to use any skill that positively helps to communicate what I am feeling when I get to about a 4 to solve any potential issues before they become a problem. That is why you must know what your triggers are so they can be avoided as much as possible. (I had to take anger management twice to figure that out.)

Nonviolent communication. Nonviolent communication is a practice developed by Marshall Rosenberg, PhD and breaks down your feelings in needs being met or not. When needs are not being met, the fear you have causes angry feelings to continue until they explode. It basically comes down to how you feel and how to express that feeling in a way that brings solutions to everyone involved so that they feel heard. Check out *Nonviolent Communication* by Marshall Rosenberg; that book is a life saver.

Breathing and meditation. There is a spiritual aspect to anger management that often goes overlooked. You have to go deeper inside to figure out why you are angry. The answers to your anger are within you, and only you have the keys to unlock that answer. If you are living with the wounds of abandonment, you might be anxious if someone stands you up and becomes angry. You may be upset because they did not value your time, but in truth, issues with abandonment issues are being triggered. It is up to you to breathe through that moment to understand that difference. Whether you were betrayed by someone close to you or a stranger rear-ended your brand-new vehicle, making the time to meditate and breathe can give you time to react and find a suitable solution for everyone involved. Many people worry that you must spend hours on end in the lotus position, but studies have shown five to ten minutes to quiet your mind, twice a day is ideal in a daily practice will do wonders for your well-being. Do not worry if it takes a while to do this and your mind still wanders. If you build it, it will come.

Redirection

Colleen M. Canestrari
Family Legacy: United States Army,
United States Air Force & United States Navy

Regain control and re-direct your life.

I wish I could tell each one of you that it will pass. That feeling of helplessness, loss of control, the overwhelming sense that you are alone in this feeling you are having. The problem with anxieties and depressions is that they convince you that you are, in fact, alone. That no one will understand what you are going through, that you will seem crazy if you talk about it, that you will be judged somehow for being a broken human being, when in reality what you are going through is a very human and common experience. This is especially the case after going through traumatic events or injuries, but is also present in everyday civilian life.

Your heart is racing, you cannot breathe. You feel like you may faint, or even die right there where you stand. You are in the middle of a grocery store and no one here knows you, would help you, would know what you are going through. You are frozen; all you want to do is escape this moment. These thoughts are paralyzing and all too common with many types of anxiety. The problem with these attacks being thoughts is that visually, everyone around you may think you are fine. If you do not voice it, strangers will just assume nothing is wrong. You are standing alone, trying to accomplish an everyday task and you feel completely unable to function. The good news is (and yes, even in this terrible moment there is good), there are tools you can use to help pull yourself out of this and accomplish your task, grab your groceries, and go about your day.

One of the most difficult (for me) yet important things to embrace is that you have power over these thoughts. Though they may still occur from time to time, or worse, you may anticipate them (a la "pre-anxiety"), they never have to be as bad or as long-lasting as they once were. Years ago, after over a year of talk therapy visits once per week, I took away a couple particularly useful tools (requiring zero actual tools or therapy visits) that greatly eased my anxious thoughts.

The first: Firetruck. Yes, really. Bear with me. You are beginning to feel stress and anxiety build. Imagine these feelings as actual tangible things. For this exercise, there is a firetruck. Horn blaring, a 5-alarm fire somewhere across town. You know it is coming based on how loud it is. You also know, it will get louder before it passes. Do you hear it louder as it is coming closer and yet... there it goes? The moment and the anxiety have passed. Deep breath in, deep breath out.

The second: Counting. This one requires a little patience and, let us be real—the items here can be interchangeable for whatever works for you in the moment. This one is great for not only getting past an anxious moment but also redirecting your thoughts to tangible things. The familiar feeling of dread builds in your mind and you know the anxious and traumatic feelings or memories are right behind it.

Take one moment to acknowledge that you are aware of it, then find five things you can see. Yes, literally, right in front or around you. For me, right this moment it is a cup of water, a dog, a laptop, a phone, and a magazine. Next, four things you can hear. I hear my dog snoring, my typing, traffic a street away and the washing machine. Three things you can touch. The plastic keyboard, a warm blanket, and my scruffy dog. Two things you can smell. Coffee from this morning and a candle nearby. One thing you can taste. I taste the ice-cold water from my cup. There. We are now many, many thoughts past the anxious ones. Your mental exercises that redirect your thoughts can have such positive and lasting effects on managing anxiety.

Lastly, a bonus tool. Imagine your anxious thoughts are an actual physical item that you can see in front of you. You know it is there. You see it clearly. You accept its existence, and you move on. You put it on the bookshelf. You may be able to still see it, but can also walk by, move on with your day, and accomplish all that you've set out to do.

Warrior Chant

MSgt Brice R Snyder
United States Marine Corps

Create a Warrior mantra for your faith, family, health, well-being, and ultimate performance.

"If everything becomes the priority, nothing is a priority!" I can still hear my Platoon Sergeant making me repeat that statement while gasping for air. My 70-inch, 160-pound frame hauling the 2nd Squad's 240 machine gun and 45-pound A.L.I.C.E. pack strapped tightly on my back through the never-ending, dusty trail-ridden mountains at Camp Pendleton, CA.

As with all newly minted Marines, practical phrases turned into warrior chants and would be forcefully drilled into the mind through the continuous "repeat after me" call and response at the highest volume one could muster, in every clime and place imaginable. (Our Platoon Sergeant's particular favorite location for reciting warrior chants happened to be outside of the Officer's quarters at 0500 during morning PT.)

It still amazes me that over 20 years later I find myself still regurgitating that very same statement almost daily in some facet, only now the student has become the teacher. I spend my days passing this onto my SNCOs. Of course, the repetitive "warrior chant" style of teaching while climbing mountains with excessive gear and a slew of weaponry slung over their backs is a thing of the past, replaced now with PowerPoint presentations, scribbled notes recorded in little "green monster" style notepads, and italicized statements captured in the signature line in all of my emails. Even still, the principal message remains the same: "If everything is the priority, nothing is a priority".

It is from this valuable lesson, carried with me throughout my career, that my "Warrior Life Hack" was hatched. As a Marine, I have been driven by the principal idea that I must always be striving for more, forever in the pursuit of higher success. There is an always-looming, "Never settle for what I am today, always do more, and always be pushing myself to a higher level" (insert any other cliché motivational slogan, here) expectation that comes with the title. An expectation of Peak Performance, always, commonly referred to as: "The Warrior Mentality."

Although I agree that a healthy level of warrior mentality is necessary to keep that internal drive alive, I have also realized that operating at peak performance, or even attempting to, always has led to failure. Even warriors need to recover. Time and time again, through the continuous "pursuit of excellence", I have fallen short. More importantly, I have left in my path a never-ending trail of disappointment, broken promises, and fractured relationships amongst the individuals and actual priorities surrounding me. I believe that it is fair to say that I am not alone on this concept. Commitment to Country and Service takes a level of drive and sacrifice few will ever understand or care to attempt. For those in it, it becomes an expectation and the norm.

Late into my career, as things just outside of my sphere of control began to spiral downward and I realized that those already-damaged relationships had become far too fractured, I knew my focus was lost. I had reached a low point in my career, in my life, and it was somewhere in this moment that those same words I uttered on that mountain side so long ago came to light. I took an audible pause and began to inventory the priorities, needs, relationships, and activities in my life. In this moment came the realization that I simply had way too many "things" in my life. I was "unbalanced."

I needed to make a significant change to the way I prioritized everything. I needed to regain balance. To begin the corrective procedures, I utilized a simple concept: I created an imaginary foundation. This imaginary foundation (like any four-cornered structure) is made up of four cornerstones, the steadfast and solid anchor points which the entire structure depends on for stability. Through some internal meditation, categorizing, and deep thought, I assigned four major priorities in my life to serve as those four cornerstones.

My specific cornerstones are:

1. **Faith**: Service and time spent with my God.

2. **Family**: Service and time invested in my Wife, my Children, my Marines, and my close personal friends.

3. **Health and well-being**: My time and actions devoted to "my temple" (my body and my mind).

4. **Performance**: Time invested in my work and daily requirements.

These cornerstones arguably could be different for anyone individual depending on their own personal circumstances, feelings, and goals. The importance lies within one's ability to identify and assign their "True Priorities." Removing what appears to be "important" and defining in your own life what truly matters (this may take some time) and is the precise recipe for the entire concept to take shape.

With my cornerstones defined and fixed in place, I was then able to determine and implement the practical application of specific tasks and actions to be conducted daily to maintain balance within each cornerstone. In layman's terms, I created a plan that involves a cultivating a balance (time and action spent daily) that is both deliberate and intentional. I ensure the time invested in each action will positively impact the cornerstone. The key to this is balance and being intentional. When engaged in any one of my cornerstones, I ensure to mitigate any distractions and maintain direct and genuine presence in the moment. If a distraction arises, I must determine if the distraction is more important than the current time and result of my actions focused on the cornerstone. If the distraction is not as important, I remove it and return to the present moment. This has been the most significant part of the process. We as humans often tend to react to every change and distraction. Instead, focus on the task at hand must be paramount. In this case intentional and deliberate focus is spent on the truly important priority.

An example of my newfound daily plan with a balanced focus towards my priorities could look like the following:

Health and well-being. A solid gym session in the morning followed by recovery. (cell phone off, or on airplane mode to avoid unnecessary distractions)

Faith. Meditation, and prayer first thing in the morning, before anyone else is awake, and again before bed (at both times my phone is set to silent and out of my reach).

Performance. My undivided attention in my tasks and responsibilities during working hours with two scheduled breaks for breath work.

Family. Scheduled time during the day to call/text my family to see how their day is going and let them know they are important and appreciated, followed by an evening unplugged from social media, television, and any other distractions that may take time away from my family and/or pull my focus away from the moment.

This is a daily, weekly, and monthly practice. By spending time each day focused on an equal level of investment to each cornerstone, I find that I am overall more productive and fulfilled. This may sound simple, but as "the fog of war" would have it, there will often be a natural imbalance. Daily commitments and required tasks may in turn disrupt the planned actions for each cornerstone. Simply put, "life happens" and this is where difficulty and discipline must be met and mastered. On any given day, I may find that I cannot invest a balanced amount of time in each cornerstone. When this occurs, I must adjust my following day's plan to ensure more time is spent invested in a cornerstone that was neglected the day prior. I measure my balance in all four corners on a weekly basis. Each week, I reflect on the activities and actions that occurred throughout those seven days, analyze my ability to manage each cornerstone, and adjust for the week ahead based on any discrepancies or setbacks that may have occurred.

When I am balanced, I am ultimately able to remove distractions that quite honestly do not matter. I am genuinely happy, healthier, more confident, and assertive overall, and feel more productive. I still enjoy a plethora of fun and exciting activities and have professional and social relationships that are cared for and relevant in my life. I can say "no" to the things that could ultimately disrupt my balance or take away from my investment in the cornerstones and feel perfectly fine doing so. My priorities are my priorities, and my remaining responsibilities and tasks are worked around them. This has been a significantly impactful change in my life that has improved my mind, body, and spirit without question.

Thank you to all veterans and service members of our grateful nation, your sacrifice and commitment to our beloved country will never be forgotten. This is still the greatest nation in the world; your names are forever etched in its history.

Leaning Into Your Fears to Free Yourself

Monique Medved

Make positive self-talk a habit and learn your fears.

Having grown up as a granddaughter of Croatian immigrants, war has held a heavy reign over my family and upbringing. That warrior-like mentality to survive has been instilled in me ever since I was a child. However, a lot of the belief systems that were instilled in me when I was young were deeply rooted in fear.

The realization I made at 25 was that these belief systems no longer served me. I did not need to live my life in fear like my grandparents were forced to at my age. I did not need to run away from war or fight for my freedom and my right to live. Through the hard work and suffering my grandparents endured, I was allowed to lead a very privileged life, one that I will be forever grateful for.

Having been partially raised by my grandparents during the early years, that unhealed trauma they suffered filtered down to me and a lot of their values and views on life informed my early education and foundational beliefs. Meanwhile, the conflicting beliefs between my parents and grandparents left me as a confused child trying to please everyone.

But there comes a point in adulthood where you need to recognize how these types of limiting beliefs hold you back from living a fulfilling life; a time when you need to stop living with that constant fear—especially when it's not *your* fear to hold onto.

Everyone experiences fear at some point in their lives. We are creatures of habit and often shy away from being challenged to grow when we can't fully anticipate the outcome. We prefer to stay comfortable in a place that feels safe, even if this means having regrets and missed opportunities when we're older.

But while a little bit of fear is a good thing and stops you from doing crazy things, most of the time it holds you back and is often based on limiting beliefs you were conditioned to believe from a young age or the stories that you tell yourself on repeat, on endless repeat over years that have the potential to turn into decades.

So many of us are fearful of change because of the level of uncertainty it brings, but change is inevitable. You should not allow the fear of it to prevent you from embracing the unknown, remaining true to yourself and fully participating in every chapter of your life…even if there are some you would rather skip.

There are all kinds of fears that hold us back throughout life. It might be the fear of rejection, embarrassment, loss of love, loss of financial security, or loss of respect. Harboring these fears puts you on a scale of feeling pain, helplessness, depression, and worst of all paralysis. When we let our fears control and consume us, they hold us back from living our dreams and seeking fulfillment in things that give us meaning in life. But by facing them, we put ourselves on the scale of having power, choice, excitement and generally feel more healthy and productive emotions.

Having the confidence to follow your passions and participate in activities you would usually shy away from gives you back the control you feel you might have temporarily lost, ultimately making you happier.

The good news in all of this is that fears are learned. You are not born being fearful. In fact, as a child, you're generally fearless because everything is new and exciting to you. Your approach to life is generally to lead with a sense of curiosity and wonder rather than fear and expectation. But as we get older and are taught what to fear, we become bound by them—as well as the root cause of their continued power over us. That means that with a little self-discipline and practice, you have the power to overcome your fears and stop them from holding you back.

This is how you can conquer your fears and realize your full potential to move out of your own way and start living the life you have always dreamed of having.

Figure out what is holding you back. Make a list of all the things you are afraid to do. This could be things such as moving to a new city, leaving a stable job, or leaving a long-term relationship that no longer fulfils you. Or maybe it is something as simple as talking to and meeting new people.

Ask yourself, "Why am I afraid of this?" Once you have made your list, begin to think of why each statement causes feelings of fear for you. For example, you might add to, "*I'm fearful of starting my own business*" with, "*Because I'm worried that I won't make it financially and I might humiliate myself if it fails.*" Once you do this, you begin to realize that you are the one creating your fears by imagining the negative future outcome instead of focusing on the potential positive outcomes. It is the narrative behind the fear you are telling yourself that is the root of the fear itself.

Imagine the best possible scenario. Instead, take that sentence and transform it into a positive one. For example, you might say, "*I am no longer fearful of starting my own business and failing financially, because instead I will work hard and implement strategies to make my business successful. And everything is a lesson to be learnt not a* *failure to be had."* Doing this flips the fearful and helpless attitudes we have towards our fears and immediately transforms them into positive, empowering visions for success.

Use positive self-talk. Positive and powerful statements we tell ourselves allow us to create a success-oriented mindset by stating something in the now and believing it to be true. What you think, you become. So why not become something great? The next time you start to doubt an outcome, imagine the reality you desire and then form a positive statement that declares it already being achieved. For example, *"I am so happy and grateful now that I've done x, y, z."*

Change your language. By wiping "can't" from your vocabulary and acting as if you have already achieved your desirable outcome, you start to behave and think as though the outcome you want is already occurring. You begin to manifest and work towards that higher vision you have for what you want to achieve. You will find you begin to attract your desire in a particular situation, acting towards your goals. Replace negative thoughts with positive ones and visualize successful outcomes when you start to doubt yourself. And if you suddenly start to think, *"What if this does not work?"* change it and start to think instead, *"Well, what if it does?"*

Build up to bigger challenges. Starting small is often underestimated. Taking on smaller challenges and working our way up gives us the confidence needed to achieve greater growth and success in the long-term. If you want to run a marathon, start slowly with 5km runs and focus on your nutrition. Similarly, if you want to start your own business, take a step in the right direction by contacting suppliers one day or building a website and social presence first. Breaking our goals into smaller, more manageable steps stops us from feeling fearful and overwhelmed by the huge scale of them. Instead, the small milestones when accomplished is what keeps us pushing forward. By simply bringing awareness to the things you fear and asking yourself, "Why does this fear present itself to me in this way?", you're able to backtrack to where the trigger point of that fear potentially came from.

It should be refreshing to realize that fear won't ever go away. You are *always* going to experience fear whenever you take a step toward anything that is new and unknown. It is there as a protection mechanism to keep you safe. But feeling that fear and doing it anyway forces your self-esteem and self-belief to skyrocket, as you continue to prove to yourself there is more to give if you just try and do not let the fear of what *could* happen, make *nothing* happen. The more you face your fears, the smaller and more manageable they become and the happier you feel knowing you can reach your goals.

While there will always be certain situations you have no control over, what you can control is the way you choose to think about them. That is your superpower. No matter what the situation is, you will handle it because in one way or another, you have been in a similar situation where similar emotions and feelings have surfaced. And if you survived those circumstances, why can't you survive this one too?

I think the willingness to experience discomfort is the most valuable skill a person can have. Because it's outside of your comfort zone where you will meet a version of yourself you haven't met yet.

And at the end of the day, life does not get easier; *you* just get better. Fear is only ever a product of the thoughts you create, and the sooner you accept that fear, doubt and hesitation won't ever disappear, the easier it becomes to understand where the trigger points for those fears stem from and also how-to better cope when they do surface and you are presented with a situation that requires you to embrace the fear, lean into it and face it head-on. When we have a better understanding of what scares us and why finding ways to manage or cope with fear becomes easier.

Filling your cup with experiences, specifically ones that require you to step out of your comfort zone forces you into new and unfamiliar territories because getting out of your comfort zone from time to time alters your brain's tolerance to change, for the better. Shaking things up every now and again shows your brain that there is nothing to fear—you'll be fine on the other side of a little stress, and it will be worth it. So many of us are fearful of change because of the level of uncertainty it brings, but that change is inevitable.

The more you face your fears, the smaller and more manageable they become and the happier you feel knowing you are fully capable of reaching new heights.

There are three simple facts of life:

1. If you do not go after what you want, you will never have it.

2. If you do not ask, well then, the answer will always be no.

3. If you do not take just one step forward, you will be in the same place forever. And isn't that scarier than taking just one step forward in a new direction?

Trauma keeps you in a loop of your past. Which is why you will find yourself in a 26-year-old's body with a 6-year-old's mindset and thought process. That is why we people please and constantly seek validation from everything and anyone outside of ourselves. We revert to that inner child that is screaming for someone to validate their existence and make them feel safe. It is even why we find ourselves staying in places longer than we need to because that certainty is what we need to feel safe and not afraid.

We seek certainty in comfort. So, get comfortable with the fact that the only certain thing in life is that one day it all comes to an end. Let that be your drive to strive for a life that is fully lived because you learn to live by simply living.

Embrace Extremes

Charissa Schmidt
Licensed Professional Counselor

Make a regular habit to face the difficult things you are avoiding in life.

It has been said that all great leaders are great horsemen. In my counseling practice and my work with horses, I am faced with extreme states of fear, panic, anger, excitement, and joy, yet the art and practice of horsemanship requires one to stay present with extremes. It is commonly understood that horses mirror their riders in their outward states. They can tune into and reflect our deepest unconscious drives and desires.

Whether it be by our family, our society or in the military, we are taught to hide our instincts from others. Yet horses are designed to read others to such a fine degree as a survival mechanism. Imagine a mountain lion, poised to pounce. The mountain lion is a master of hiding its true intentions. It can lay hidden in the grass, outwardly calm, all the while coiled to strike, chase and pounce. As prey animals, horses need to be able to read others to ensure their survival. Horses are sensitive enough to sense the unexpressed intention of the mountain lion before it attacks. We may be able to hide from other humans, but not from a horse. They will pick up on the angry thought that goes unexpressed, the shift in our heart rate and breathing, the slightest muscle twitch before we are conscious of ourselves.

If you can, try to remember a time when you felt well. Maybe it was in a meditation practice or a time of prayer. Maybe it was in a moment of connection to nature or people you love and care about. Wellness feels great. It means our system has not detected any threats in our environment. Again, if you can imagine what it may feel like to be a horse fighting off a mountain lion attack: imagine the amount of energy it takes to fight and run from danger. Imagine your heart rate increasing, your breath becoming more rapid. Now imagine a moment where the lion has pinned a horse and the horse knows it does not have the strength to continue. The horse may fall into a state of deep surrender and collapse.

In the mental health field, we (perhaps wrongly) call those instinctual states "mental health symptoms." Running may look like avoidance, anxiety, and restlessness. The fight instinct may look like anger, aggression, hypertension, and general irritability. The collapse state (a state we fall into when things feel hopeless) may look like depression, chronic fatigue, and dissociation.

In nature, if the attack is uninterrupted the horse will regain energy, stand up, then shake it off. The shaking is literally the nervous system resetting itself. Our modern human society does not allow our bodies to fully expel the energy that builds up in our nervous system after we are exposed to a threat. Many of us are holding onto tension from a lifetime of stress. There is an understanding that animals do not get traumatized if they can complete the cycle of run/fight, collapse, shake it off. Because we have a highly developed cerebral cortex humans get stuck.

Just as a horse may run from or attack a predator, master horsemen are able to work with extreme states of instinct. The primal human nervous system is wired in a similar way to run, fight, freeze, and if all else fails collapse. We all enjoy the feeling of being regulated, congruent and well.

If you think about a horse in a peaceful state, they may do simple things like eat, sleep and move from one place to another.

They create social groups, they engage in play, they groom and massage each other. We can help our bodies engage our instinctual resiliency through movement and connection as well. Master horse people can ride out the instincts to run, fight or collapse. They can shake off the past and return to the present moment after a threat. They understand how to allow emotional states to move through their nervous system without judgment.

When in doubt, move. Shake it off and move.

Retrain Your Brain

Kortney Yasenka, LCMHC
Licensed Clinical Mental Health Counselor, owner
of Yasenka Counseling and Coaching, LLC

Make use of cognitive restructuring techniques to help increase positive thinking.

How do you motivate yourself to live each day in a positive mindset? Things are easier said than done so how do you start living a better life? A happier life? A mentally healthier life? Does simply hanging posters on a wall help? Is it best to recite daily positive affirmations? The short answer is yes. We are all capable of living a happier life.

Here is how.

Research shows that just seeing the word "no" can change your brain, and not for the better. Think about that for a moment. Simply looking at a word can negatively impact your brain. Imagine if "no" and other negative words are not only seen but also said by you or to you daily. Negativity literally changes the wiring of your brain and causes you to not only see situations more pessimistically, but also causes you to view future situations with a negative mind set.

Now, think of your brain as having different pathways. Each pathway involved contains an automatic response to a situation caused by specific thoughts about that situation. These thoughts can be influenced by past experiences, either good or bad.

Think of it like this: every day, you take the same path to get from your back door to your shed. Every day you walk the same path, back and forth, getting to and from your house to your shed. Over time, this pathway gets more and more defined—clearer to see every day and with every traversal. This is what happens in your brain. Without even giving it a second thought, you know what pathway you will take to get to the shed. Similarly, your brain knows what pathway it will take given a situation. Unfortunately, many of us get stuck on an extremely negative path. Good news is, it's never too late to start on a new path. A new journey toward positivity.

Now, imagine you take a new route to the shed. You decided to try out a new path. What happens the first day? The terrain may be slightly rougher, and it may be more difficult for you to get to the shed. You can get there, but it takes more effort and conscious decisions on your part. The new path is not yet clearly defined. As with your brain, and creating new pathways, it will not happen overnight. It takes constant effort and practice to create new pathways. So how do you create new pathways in the brain to set yourself in a more positive direction? The answer is positive thinking.

Positive thinking is a simple concept that can produce significant results. The first step in living a better, happier, and mentally healthier life is through positive thinking.

Mind over matter is a popular saying. I like to say, "You can't always change the situation, but you can always change how you think and feel about it." Psychiatrist Aaron Beck, the father of cognitive behavioral psychology, is credited with developing theories of how changing your cognitions or thoughts can change your feelings and behaviors. A simple way to understand this is to think of a situation.

Example: Tomorrow, it is going to snow. That is the situation. Now identify the first thought that pops into your mind. For some, the automatic response would be, "No, I hate snow! Why do I live in New England?" These negative cognitions then influence your feelings, leading you to feel frustrated, disappointed, or annoyed. These feelings then in turn affect your behaviors and how you act. If you do not want to feel upset about the snow and let it ruin the day and others around you, you need to change your thoughts.

The easiest way to change how you feel about a situation is to use positive thinking. So, what could you say to yourself that would lead you down a more positive path? Instead of thinking "No, I hate snow! Why do I live in New England?" You could say, "If it snows it will be a good day to clean the house." Or, "The snow does look pretty when it falls, and it would be nice to have a relaxing day at home." If you change your automatic thought to a more positive one, it will then change how you feel and how you behave. Instead of being frustrated, disappointed, and annoyed, you might feel more relaxed and content. Your feelings will then make you behave less irritated, and you will be less irritable. It is going to snow whether you want it to or not, so you might as well make the most of it and try to be positive.

Now, I know positive thinking appears to be much easier said than done, but you have to commit to it and repeat those positive thoughts to yourself. You may not believe the thoughts, but it is important that you continue to use positive thinking. When you replace your negative thoughts with positive thoughts you create new pathways in your brain...new, more positive pathways that in time will become your automatic way of responding and thinking.

So why is maintaining a positive outlook on life so difficult for some and easier for others? Both nature and nurture play a role, but what happens when your brain has been trained to automatically respond to situations in a cautious, negative manner? That is exactly what happens to individuals who are constantly put in high-risk situations that often come down to making life or death decisions. Being in stressful situations most has an impact on the way the brain is wired. Research shows that traumatic stress can be associated with lasting changes in the brain. This means that being exposed to a traumatic event can alter your brain's pathways. This can be extremely beneficial when you are on a battlefield but can have detrimental effects on your everyday life after your service.

Most people find it doable—even relatively easy—to use positive thinking when it comes to finding the good in a potential snowstorm. But what happens when your brain is trained in a different way? The brains of individuals in the military have been conditioned to always plan for the worst-case scenario, to always be alert and to react without thinking. Active military members do not have the luxury of time or changing their automatic cognitions to positive thoughts. Again, an especially useful and helpful way of thinking when you are literally fighting for your life and others. But when you leave that lifestyle, your body may be in a new environment, but your brain, sadly, is not.

So, here are some life hacks/tips for warriors that can be used in your daily life to begin to retrain your brain, use more positive thinking, and begin living a happier and mentally healthier, better life.

3 Good Things. Every night before bed, remembers one good thing that happened during your day. This can be anything big or small that made you smile, laugh, or feel happy during your day. Recall one new thing that you did. This can be as small as if you wore a new pair of socks or tried a new hobby and thought about one thing for which you are grateful.

3 Positives for 1 Negative. Studies show that it takes anywhere between three to five positive thoughts to replace one negative thought. When you notice your automatic thought is negative, think of three positive alternatives to that situation to help change your outlook.

Happy Hour. Carve out a specific time each day to share with your family, friends, or support system, the best parts of your day. Being able to share your positive experiences with others will not only boost your wellbeing but also the wellbeing of those around you.

Positivity Poster. Create a visual of positive sayings, quotes, words, affirmations, etc. Keep this positivity poster in a place that you can see and refer to every day. Just as negative words can affect our mood, positive words can too.

Personal Mantra. Develop a personal mantra or phrase that you can repeat to yourself to help increase positivity and mental stability. Your mantra should be personal to you and incite a feeling of calmness and happiness. Write down your personal mantra or phrase on a small piece of paper and always keep it in with you. This can serve as a small reminder in times of stress and negativity.

Remember the 3 Rs. The goal is to retrain, recondition, and restructure your brain. The idea of this may be scary to some, uncomfortable and unnatural for others, but there is nothing a warrior cannot handle. With discipline, resilience, and a little hope, all virtues held by warriors, a more positive mindset is truly obtainable.

PART II

TACTICS FOR SELF-CARE

T HE DALAI LAMA said, "If you want others to be happy, practice compassion. If you want to be happy, practice compassion." Self-compassion is a type of positive disposition that allows one to speak to oneself kindly and respectfully. These activities include caring for your vessel (mind and physical body) with absolute dignity and respect.

Why does self-compassion matter?

The most important relationship outside friends and family is the one that you have with yourself. Whatever you highlight with your actions and language is the spectacle you are putting on for yourself and others. Be sure to choose wisely. For some, you may not be ready to treat yourself well; the very concept may seem incomprehensible. Hopefully, when you are ready, you will return to the following content when you are *not* making a regular habit of mishandling yourself. When you do return, return with an open mind. Understand that if you want your reality to change, please know that you may change it at any time.

Some things for you to think about as you proceed are:

1.   How you are reframing your personal actions?

2.   Are you watching the language you use to speak to yourself?

The contributors in the following chapters have provided a wide array of tactics and they are actively engaged in putting them into play to take care of themselves. These tactics are very deliberate and purposeful. Benas' self-compassion tactic, for example, is making a regular habit to play golf, spending time with his wife, two golden retrievers, hiking, and reading books. His living space is also dominated by lots of house plants that he is struggling to cultivate. Benas is also deliberate to avoid negative self-talk and makes a point of avoiding oversharing of personal thoughts/ opinions and judgment in most of his conversations. He has adopted the Marine Corps boot camp ditty of counting down from tens and fives to quickly transition an event and re-engage the brain. This counting down helps him snap into focus, strip away the judgment and negative thoughts.

Buzz makes a daily habit of running long distances with his wife and making a regular practice of fitness. His exercise routine is sprinkled with lots of variety and experimentation with new movements. He also loves cooking, reading, and spending time with his family. Self-care and resiliency are expectations and measures of competition in the Bryan houschold. To recharge for respite, Buzz, and his wife love to travel.

Power Couple

Lieutenant Colonel Ross "RAW" Hobbs
United States Air Force

Ashton Cantou
Certified Transformational Life Coach and
Leadership Coach for High Performance

Become a lifelong observer and a learner.

Ashton Cantou

Adopt a CEO (Compassionate, Empowered Observer) perspective. Here's the deal. You are not your thoughts; you *have* thoughts. You are not your emotions, you *have* emotions. You are not your actions, you *act*.

We too often get wrapped up in over-identifying with things like feelings and failure. One of the greatest opportunities for empowered growth comes from your ability to take on a CEO perspective: that of a Compassionate, Empowered Observer. You must learn to witness and observe yourself and others without making judgments. You can begin to turn down the volume on your inner analyzer through breathwork and meditation, just so you can see how you show up to life without over analyzing or over-identifying. This includes deciding to view yourself and all people with compassion, which starts with recognizing that every act is either an act of love or a cry for it.

Finally, choose to see all thoughts, emotions, and actions as feedback to gain more clarity about who you want to be and what you want to create in your life. From the CEOs perspective, there is no failure, only feedback. There is less right or wrong, and more emphasis placed on what is effective and ineffective. With this vantage point, you can simply witness who or what is no longer serving you and your life, then from an empowered stance make a more effective choice about who you want to be and what you want to create.

Radical responsibility. I am bringing this up second because it must be done without guilt, shame, or judgment. For the sake of being 100 percent real with you, the truth is that we are *always* in a state of choice. Of course, terrible things do happen. Pain is inescapable but suffering and rumination are our choice. When we choose to take radical responsibility for our lives, we take ownership of our lives. We take our power back by owning that we are in control of our experience of and response to the events that take place in our lives. Radical responsibility is the elimination of *all* blame, the death of the ego, and the annihilation of a victim mentality. It says I am in choice, no matter what; I am playing a role in this relationship or situation and no one or nothing has the power to decide how I think, feel, or act but me.

Feel, deal, and heal. The only way out is through. This step comes once you are ready to own and face your stuff. When you are truly tired of suffering. It is the messy part of the journey. It is the darkness, shame, guilt, trauma, regrets, and resentments. To feel, you must accept the truth of what has happened and face your demons. You must look at your deepest pain and shame straight in the face. You must own your weakness. You must create room to allow the most unbearable and uncomfortable feelings to flow through you. It takes courage and may be the hardest thing you ever do. For most people, pain is buried deep beneath the surface in the subconscious. In the military, you are conditioned to believe that feelings or emotions will get you killed. While this may be true on the battlefield, it is 100 percent necessary to process emotions off the battlefield.

My advice does whatever it takes to shed what is weighing you down. This will take humility. Examples of help could include psych-therapy, hypno-therapy, EMDR therapy, somatic therapy, life coaching, or support groups. Find your medicine and get the roots of your pain. Pull them up and plant new more empowering belief systems about who you are and what is possible for your life. Always remember- The past is not what defines us, but instead helps to guide us for a better present and future.

Create a vision. When one chapter of your life ends and a new one begins, there is a huge void to be filled. A grief can take over that few acknowledge, and a lack of clarity sets in. It can feel like you have lost your whole identity. Once again, there is an opportunity here to create a life by design. How?

Look at your longings and discontents. Where are you longing for more? Do you desire love, freedom, success? Where are you discontented? Are you unhappy with your health, job, or relationship? List these things out. Define exactly what would light you up instead. What would bring you the most joy? Figure out who you need to become to bring that vision to life and create a plan of action to achieve it.

The power of the pivot. This one is simple and profound. These are our catalyst moments. An opportunity to expand or shrink back when life brings an unexpected roadblock or twist.

This is taking a failure and turning it into a steppingstone. Taking a broken relationship and using it as a catalyst for your evolution. No matter what life throws your way you can leverage it to your advantage. Do not pick up the ball and quit. Keep your eyes on the goal and pivot your way to the finish line.

Always remember:

Surrender is a power move. We believe that God is in control, that there is a greater plan at work, and that many times life will bring you to a place of surrender. Do not resist submitting your need for control. When you surrender you allow room spirit to work in your favor.

Leverage the power of support. Find someone you can trust to be fully open and transparent with. We are conditioned to stuff everything down and power through. Healing comes through finding a safe place to land, express, and often at the offering of a helping hand.

Self-care is non-negotiable. Everything is touching. Your mental, physical, and spiritual health are all intertwined. Discipline is the ultimate sign of self-care; self-care is the ultimate sign of self-love. When you fill your cup, choose yourself, and put your wellbeing first everything in your life will be impacted positively.

Living in integrity. Align your life to your core values. So many people are living a life that is out of alignment with what truly matters to them and then they wonder why they are unhappy. It is not hard to make decisions once you know what your values are. Define and align with your own inner knowing. Do your absolute best to live in integrity with your values and your life will be full.

Lt. Col Ross "RAW" Hobbs

Meditation is where it is at. I know what you might be thinking—which is exactly what I used to think when someone would talk about meditation: "Umm, nah, I'm good, thanks," or, "I'm not into that type of weird stuff." Like most major changes we make in our lives, they take place after an extremely traumatic experience. I can say in full honesty that meditation has changed my life. When life gets hectic or when my mind gets so cluttered by negative thoughts, I turn to meditation. It is as simple as finding a quiet place, devoid of all distractions, and focusing on slowly breathing. If you feel like your mind is a battlefield or a place where you are constantly reminded of the pain and trauma from past situations, meditation clears all of that out. Believe it: meditation has been proven through MRIs to change the neuropath ways of the mind, which if you are like me, is needed. Give it a try, you will not regret it.

Physically fit to RISE! Physical fitness gives you the ability to endure and excel when others cannot. Incredibly early in my life, I started a consistent regime of running, lifting weights, and stretching 3 to 4 times a week. I can honestly say that it has been part of the foundation upon which most of my success in the US Air Force is grounded. If you have been in the military, you have likely experienced physically challenging circumstances that 99 percent of civilians will never experience or fully grasp. Flying 10+ hour combat missions, working 60+ hour weeks on minimal sleep, being expected by leadership to perform at the highest level after being awake for 24 hours straight, etc....what I have learned is that the demands of life don't impact everyone the same. Those who are more physically fit can sustain operations longer than those who are not. Those who are physically fit can think more clearly when others are confused. Those who are physically fit can lead during chaos when others are falling down.

Taking care of your body is never about the short-term benefits or passing a PT test, but instead for the moments that are unseen and unexpected. Take care of your body physically and you will rise above the rest with strength, clarity, and endurance.

Become a life-long learner. Be a life-long learner. Being a life-long learner and developing an intention for personal growth is not just about reading a book a day or going to leadership seminars. Sure, those can be part of the picture, but there is so much more to it. The desire for personal growth is fueled by the mindset you carry with you to always pay attention to what you do not know. The beautiful and frustrating part of being a life-long learner is that you are consistently shown how much you really do not know. Instead of becoming overwhelmed at the mountain of the unknown, take small steps every day. Set aside 15 to 30 minutes a day to go outside your current knowledge level and comfort bubble.

An example of what I like to do: watch a YouTube video on something I know nothing about (i.e., What is it like to hike Mt. Everest?). Just a quick word of caution: always check the source for the information to ensure it is a reliable and relevant source! Be critical; the internet can be a great place for information, but it can also provide a lot of untrue or biased information.

We truly hope that these warrior life hacks bring you peace, healing, and clarity as you continue the path to living a thriving and fulfilling life.

If you remember only three things, hold onto these:

- Surrendering control is the ultimate power move. There is no use in attempting to control the things you cannot control, which as it turns out is much of what we all encounter.

- There must be an alignment of values between your physical, mental, emotional, and spiritual health.
- Keep moving forward. Even the tiniest step in the right direction is better than standing still. Do not be overwhelmed, just know that you are capable of all things and greatness takes time. As you have probably heard, "Rome wasn't built in a day."

Morning Routine

Dani Rocco
Mother of a U.S. Marine,
Devoted to a Soldier **podcast**

Structure your day with a morning routine that will set your day right.

It's my belief that we are meant to continuously grow, learn, evolve, challenge ourselves, fail, and learn to love to fully maximize our lives. That means to love to the fullest, you must be willing to feel pain in its fullest. You cannot live into your purpose without each emotion. You also cannot fully appreciate the love you have for yourself or experience love from others or give love without both emotions.

So much of our life is spent running from pain and uncomfortable feelings. We are running from our true happiness and love. Happiness, joy, passion, fulfillment is aligned and visually speaking holding hands with sadness, pain, lack. How do we embrace our pain? How do we forget and not let it haunt us? How do we let go of guilt? How do we forgive? How do we learn to love all the ugly and brilliance of who we are? How do we love someone else without the fear or judgement? How do we lead with love? It starts with you. Looking at who you are. How are you living and thinking? How are you applying the lessons you learn? How much responsibility of your life are you accepting and how much are you deflecting?

How do I personally evolve my life to lead with love? I look to history. I learn from others' history and my own. In those examples, I apply new habits, evolve the ones I have, confront my faults and fears. Then I look how I can apply that to my relationships with others. It always starts with me. I can't lead with love and fully give and receive love if I'm hiding behind my personal excuses and pain.

This is exactly how I do it. I personally use scripture, but you can use philosophy, motivational videos/books, theory... anything that you resonate with.

Every morning, I do these five things in this order:

1. Before I get out of bed, I pray for how I want to feel that day, how I want my day to go and anything else that is on my heart.

2. I read from scripture.

3. I reflect and then decide how I am going to apply it in my life or what I need to learn from it.

4. I read a devotional specific to that scripture.

5. I write in my journal, using the following prompts:

    a. How do I need to apply what I read to me personally?

    b. How I can apply it to my relationships?

    c. Lastly, I end with letting myself own whatever fears, judgment, or pain I'm experiencing—basically, anything negative that comes up. I take those negative thoughts and I rewrite as if I have already mastered how I want to feel and how I want my life in those situations to be.

As I go through my day, I can pull from that morning as a reminder of where I am going, my worth and the desires that

I can achieve. I do not need to worry or be in pain because I have the reminder of my truth, the truth, and the love I give to myself and others.

There are many tools and resources to pick from; one is not righter than the other. Some tools or resources might work for a while but as you evolve your tools and resources need to evolve with you. Design and use what "calls" to you. Be brave and explore. You know the outcome 100 percent of one thing in life, changing nothing will keep you exactly feeling and where you are today.

Having this routine reminds me of my truth—my truth in myself and my truth in my relationships. It stops the lies that form in my mind about who I am and how I feel. Facts are facts. Somedays are harder than others and I must remind myself cautiously and other days not at all. Nothing happens overnight. Everything worth having in your life comes with time, practice, and dedication. Short cuts only build a weak foundation. Plug in to the Warrior Life Hacks that resonate and remember: "This is not how your story will end."

Be Deliberate in Your Preparation for Each Day

James Smith
United States Army, Green Beret

"A goal without a plan is just a wish.
    —ANTOINE DE SAINT-EXUPERY

Be deliberate in your
preparation for each day.

We all live busy and sometimes complicated lives. Are you able to stay focused? Can you accomplish your tasks with the numerous distractions our lives give us? I have a problem with both things (maybe because my attention span is almost nonexistent), but there's good news! We have and are well versed in the problem-solving skills we need to identify and solve any set of issues that eventually lead to mission success. But how do we break it down?

Think back to a mission statement in an operations order. To us, that mission statement was the most important thing on that document and accomplishing it was a no-fail event...but to our higher headquarters, it was just a small objective in the overarching plan. Guess what: it is no different now. The only difference is that we are our *own* higher headquarters, and it is *our* overarching plan.

Now, let me bring my friends "implied and specified tasks" into the mix. Once we have a clearly defined dream or end goal, we can begin to identify the implied and specified tasks we need to accomplish to achieve mission success. The great thing is that we can also use these tasks as progress markers for how close or far we are from accomplishing our wildest dreams and goals.

It is important to mention that this process is also where you can empower yourself or beat yourself to death. Use your accomplishments (or failures) to congratulate yourself and to learn from your mistakes, this will help you stay on course and to keep up your momentum in the day-to-day grind. You may find that you have achieved something amazing and that it morphed while you were in this phase which is why it is so important to conduct progress checks daily, weekly, monthly, quarterly, etc.

If you are working with a team, I highly encourage you to pay attention to these milestones being reached. You will find out more about yourself and you will be pleasantly surprised to watch your colleagues crush something that is outside of their wheelhouse which only makes your organization stronger.

Whether you are the CEO of a Fortune 500 company or a low man in a ditch digging outfit, our days should start the same: by investing time in ourselves. I tackle this with a "whole of wellness" approach that includes devotional time with my Creator, physical exercise, fellowship with my accountability partner(s), and with the help of my calendar, mentally preparing myself for the events on it.

Be deliberate in your day's preparation and be fully present in whatever task you are working on. If you do this your day will be less stressful and more productive for you and your organization. Also, and this is especially important. Understand and accept that Murphy will hit you when you least expect it, and this could cause a huge derailment in your process. It is at this moment that you must extend a huge heap of grace towards your colleagues and yourself! I know how frustrating this can be, but we can either accept what has happened and use it as a learning lesson or allow ourselves to completely derail our project while it circles the drain.

Just as the above mentioned quote reminds us, a plan could fail but adding the art of planning to your life is a key to success that is too often overlooked.

Start Your Day with a Sense of Calm

Corin Cunningham
Healthcare Manager

It is profound self-care to get up in the morning and start your day with a sense of calm.

When your alarm first goes off, your initial reaction or habit might be to hit snooze, roll over, and catch a few more precious minutes of sleep. *Don't do this.* I have found this to be extremely tempting, but in my experience, it leads to grogginess and makes it even harder to get out of bed. Instead, try this quick five-minute energizing meditation right from your bed.

When your alarm goes off, turn it off. Lay on your back, close your eyes, and take three slow deep breaths. Imagine a bright white light washing over you, starting at your head. As you are imagining this light, make sure you are taking deep, intentional breaths. Picture the light slowly moving down your entire body from the top of your head down to your toes, energizing you for your day. Continue with this visualization for about 1 to 3 minutes, or whatever feels right to you. Counting backwards from 60 to 1 is a great way to keep time while you are doing this. When you feel ready, take three final deep breaths, open your eyes, and get ready to face your day.

Sleep Hygiene

Heike Sommers
Psychiatric Mental Health Nurse
Practitioner, military family

Make sound and healthy sleep a priority.

I think of sleep as a pillar of mental health. Sleep deprivation is a torture method for good reason, and oftentimes we contribute to that ourselves. Add in PTSD from real torture and combat or vicarious trauma to the mix and sleep becomes a farfetched, seemingly impossible notion.

The obvious do's and don'ts to improve sleep are:

Laying off the screen time at least 2 hours before bedtime. More, if you can, but this gives your brain time to unwind and settle down before sleep.

No alcohol in the evening. Alcohol turns into fat and sugar and has a short half-life, meaning it will wake you up in the early morning hours.

No cannabis. The use of cannabis might help you to relax, but will not help you stay asleep.

Physical activity. Help your body to be tired by exercising in the earlier parts of the day and go for another walk after dinner.

Respect your sleeping space. Bedrooms are for sleep only; if you must work from home, do not use your bedroom if you have any sleep issues at all.

Investigate any health concerns that might be affecting your quality of sleep. If you snore and wake up gasping for air, please get a sleep consultation with a specialist to rule out sleep apnea.

Try incorporating meditation. Meditation is great, as if you can manage to be in the moment, there is no anxiety—anxiety happens in the past or future. Not everyone likes sitting meditations, but it can be fun to meditate with family and friends. Movement meditations are another option. There are great apps for sleep, such as the Cognitive Behavioral Therapy app called CBT-I (among many others).

Try natural sleeping solutions. Medications can be a good temporary solution for chronic insomnia. Sometimes, people develop anxiety about not sleeping and it becomes a vicious cycle that needs to be broken. Natural solutions are a good first choice, like melatonin, Valerian root, ashwagandha and the old tried-and-true milk and cookie routine when you wake up. However, in cases with serious symptoms of PTSD it might be a good idea to talk with your health care provider about Trazodone (a good and non-habit-forming sleeping medication), Gabapentin, or even a hypnotic for the short term if you are struggling with intense nightmares and flashbacks. Prazosin is an alpha blocker that can be helpful as well in suppressing nightmares.

Have a sleep ritual. Transitioning into sleep can be easier with rituals, not to mention how the burden of going through your daily schedule can be eased by instituting structure.

Creating a Sanctuary Where You Live

Gwen Lawrence
Yogi for Active-Duty Military and Veterans

Prioritize your personal space and make it your sanctuary for health and well-being.

In my experience of working with warriors, I prefer to give them ways to address all their senses. We all have different ways of manifesting PTSD and trauma, so I feel that by giving options, I stand the best chance of helping them to cope.

It is about creating a sanctuary in your own home or room, no matter what socioeconomic situation you are in. You have the power to create a space that is safe and brings complete joy.

Your eyes must be able to relax in your home. You need to execute a plan to token your home, find a place for everything, and take time in the morning to make your bed and straighten up. I know for me personally I cannot take on my day with clients or projects if I know my kitchen is a mess. Maintenance is the key. If you make one cleanup day a week it could prove to be an insurmountable task. Instead, daily maintenance and a comprehensive chore list is the way to go. Quarterly, go through your drawers, cabinets, and closets to get rid of things no longer useful for you and create space and organization that is most pleasing to your eye. You do not have to go crazy, but I guarantee you will find comfort and relaxation in an atheistically pleasing environment you can be proud of.

Smell is important in your home. Consider getting an air cleaning plant or two to refresh your oxygen in your home. Better oxygenation has been proven to lead to clearer thinking, better body function, and organ function. Consider getting some aromatherapy in the form of an oil diffuser. I like this better than candles because most candles are not only a fire risk but made with harmful chemicals. By getting a diffuser and set of oils, you can choose to set the fragrance according to your needs each day. If you are stressed and cannot sleep, for example, try lavender; if you are low energy, try orange oil; if you feel as though you may be starting to get sick, explore mints or tea tree oil. Aromatherapy is a very ancient art that utilizes the olfactory system to influence our moods and health. There are many places online where you can get free information.

Understand the importance of breathing. If you learn basic diagrammatic breathing techniques, which are essentially breathing in and out of your nose and deep into your belly, you can learn to shut down your fight or flight response and help yourself to relax, let go of stress and anxiety and take a moment of down time. Do this type of breathing for 1 to 3 minutes before getting out of bed and any time the day gets ahead of you or your anxiety is on the rise. The great thing is this type of mindfulness technique can be done anywhere, at any time, not just while lying down with your eyes shut.

Hearing seems to speak for itself. For centuries, the importance of sound vibrations on the mood have been researched and discussed. Try to choose only uplifting music that invokes positive feelings and not negative memories. Instead of the TV, turn on your favorite tunes and watch the mood change, the body lighten, and just plain have fun. As the saying goes, dance as though nobody is watching!

Touch goes hand in hand with trying to create the home sanctuary. If you have blankets, sheets or furniture that you do not feel loved and cozy in, donate them and replace them with soft, pleasing textiles. If you can't afford new furniture, try getting large soft blankets and draping your couch or favorite chair with it. The results of a hug from your furniture is bound to relax you and suspend your stress.

Taste is a twofold practice. Of course, it goes without saying you want to feed your body right for optimum living. Always remember: garbage in, garbage out. If you are eating less-than-nutritious foods, your body cannot heal, thrive, or grow. In fact, it will have a hard time surviving and will instead feed "dis-ease". So, take the time to make great choices. There are times to have treats, but do not make it a habit. Try to eat 24 grams or less of sugar per day, half your body weight in ounces of protein per day, and drink plenty of water. As an estimate, take your body weight and multiply it by 10; that is the basic number of calories you need per day to maintain your body weight.

The other aspect of the mouth is committing to positive talk. This is important because, once again, garbage in, garbage out! If you are lying, gossiping, and participating in hurtful speech, you are attracting it all back to you. Unless you are a sociopath, those qualities are thought of as undesirable and unproductive. This can take time to learn and practice, but it is possible, and you will see amazing results.

Self-Reflection

Tara Hunter
RN and Veteran's Advocate

*Reflect on self to improve to benefit
health and relationships.*

Life is fluid: always changing and going through ebb-and-flows.
Days of highest wins and days when it feels like the weight of
the world is on one's shoulders. The key to living one's best life
is using self-reflection exercises, which are a form of self-love—
these exercises create a grounded understanding of one's values,
beliefs, and purpose. These components make up one's whole
being and allows a person to reach their inner self—creating a
true understanding of oneself and foundation for living one's
best life. This is like having a shield of defense that continues
protecting one's mental health and well-being by guiding decisions, actions, and outcomes. It can be done throughout the day
or once day with results seen over time.

The best place to do self-reflection is in a comfortable, quiet
space with no external stimuli to create distractions. It is highly
individualized—meaning everybody creates their space, time,
frequency and make it into what works best for them. It can
be done by journaling, meditation, physical exercise and/or in
nature. The goal of doing self-reflection is to look at how one
is ultimately feeling and allow yourself the opportunity to have
an open mind towards the idea of acceptance and the ability to

let go and/or develop a positive way to move forward to a more fulfilling life.

Self-reflection is powerful because it develops based on what is meaningful to a person. This is what creates life-long change by allowing a person to be fully aware of how they are feeling, accept what is going well and remove those things that are hindering their happiness. It is a time when a person can feel safe and reach down to their inner core being. By reaching this inner being, a foundation of healing, growth and strength is built. Over time, this leads to deeper healing for wounds that are buried and subconsciously affects daily life, leading to a happier existence.

Opioid Story

David Kendrick
U.S. Army

Understand and know that quitting
an addiction is an option.

In 2007, I was shot in both legs by a sniper. My left leg was shattered and my femoral artery was severed, leading to an exceedingly long stay in the hospital—three months total. Over the course of my stay in the hospital, I had two blood transfusions and 14 surgeries, during which time, I was hooked up to a morphine drip to reduce my pain. Every hour or so I would have a new dose of morphine flowing throughout my body.

After three months, I left the hospital. After being out for a week, I noticed something: I was fiending for the morphine I'd been hooked up to for the previous three months. Doctors prescribed me Vicodin to deal with the pain, and it did help—but the morphine from the hospital is what I *really* wanted.

I tried to go back to the hospital to get more surgery; I told doctors I was still having pain and I needed another procedure. But that did not work; instead, I was prescribed a strong opioid to deal with the pain I was having. That did the trick for me, as along with alcohol, I'd found a great way to get the buzz that I was looking for from the opioids.

The unit that I was assigned to at that time was called the Warrior Transition Unit. The unit was new on Ft. Carson as a place for injured soldiers to get back to a regular unit or heal from their injuries and return to civilian life. In this unit, I met a group of guys who were also injured and were also prescribed opioids for their pain.

What I found there was a secret black market of sorts, where everyone traded their opioids. If you had something that someone wanted, they would trade you what they have for what you had. Eventually, I started hanging with a group of guys that drank heavily and abused opioids just like I did. That is when I noticed something. If you hang with people who have the same addiction you have, no one will ever tell you that you have a problem.

One day, one of my good friends was going out to a bar with a separate group of friends. He asked me to come meet him at the bar after I was done hanging out downtown. At around 2 am, I met him and his friends and I was surprised at what I saw. His face was bruised and bloodied; I thought he'd gotten beat up. But one of his friends told me that he fell face first off the curb onto the ground.

When we got him back to his apartment, I stayed with him for a while, but when you see one of your friends inebriated all the time, you get to thinking that they're always going to be okay. This happened on a Saturday night. On Monday at 3 pm, I got the call that my friend was dead.

Since I was not an immediate family member, no one told me the cause of death. It could have been several factors: alcohol poisoning, a mixture of pills and alcohol, or the fall causing bleeding on the brain. All I knew for sure was that I felt like crap. My friend was dead from a death that could have been prevented if one of us in his group of friends had realized that we all had a problem.

Matters only got worse from there. My unit flew me to his hometown for his funeral, and while I was there, I met his mother. She looked me in my eyes and asked, "You were the last one with my son. Tell me what happened to him." Talk about a reality check. I felt like garbage. It was at that moment that I knew I was done abusing opioids. Seeing the ripple of emotional pain caused by opioid abuse shocked me into sobriety. I quit right then and there, cold turkey.

Today, my business Lion Speaking Agency has a mission to help individuals suffering from mental illness. The demographic includes individuals who abuse opioids to cope with their mental as well as physical pain. We are in a crisis, and it is imperative that individuals know what resources are available to them within their respective communities.

Ninjutsu: The Zen Side of Warrior Life

Stephen Suchy
United States Marine Corps

Cultivate your passion and channel your energy into a productive art that enhances your clarity and brings peace to your everyday life.

From PT to 5Ks, every veteran knows that working out can be one of the best outlets for the mental challenges that come with service. However, after years of martial arts training and meditation, I discovered working out was my form of self-medication to block out the anger I'd been holding onto well before I became a Marine.

At 13 years old, I had the unfortunate experience of finding my father dead of a heart attack. I attempted to give him CPR, not knowing my attempts were futile, and immediately became an extremely angry young man. I didn't realize *why* I was so mad—though it was probably so clear to everyone else—all I knew was that I couldn't focus enough to do anything or sleep at the end of the day unless I was exhausted. I started working out before school, going to football practice after school, and heading back to the gym after dinner for another two-hour session, usually riding my bike there and back. After getting through some homework when I got home, I would collapse into bed, completely exhausted.

I kept up this 2 to 3 workouts a day routine throughout high school and joined the Marines in my junior year after being inspired by classmates who had joined up. I found my training at Camp Lejeune challenging, and I loved that they worked me out until exhaustion, particularly at boot camp, but I would often head back to the gym at night to get in a few more hours.

I was fortunate that there were no wars on when I was in the Marines, but I volunteered for any training I came across, such as advanced communications and martial arts. I had found a connection with martial arts and never stopped training in it throughout active duty, so when I went back to New Haven and enrolled in college during my time in the reserves, I continued my martial arts training in Shotokan karate, competing on my college team and seeking more ways to exhaust my body to ensure some form of sleep.

In 1982, I was hired as a police officer and continued to feel the need for pre-sleep exhaustion—but now on a rotating schedule. Throughout my career as a direct first responder, I came across a lot of horrific things, from suicides to confrontations on SWAT to children who lost their lives tragically…all of which increased the PTSD that likely started when my father died.

A few years and two kids later, I inadvertently found a new level of martial arts training in ninjutsu when my children questioned one of my friends about his "ninja" training that he was explaining to them. After heading to the club where my friend trained, I quickly learned his sensei Greg was one of the best martial artists I had ever found or met. Greg is the one who started my Zen training; he's a warrior, but he's also a hippie. According to Greg, you become the best warrior you can so you don't have to hurt anyone—peace through superior power. Walk away if you can, but if you can't, learn how to win (but only when absolutely necessary).

Our nightly training included everything from stretching and technique to meditation and breathing exercises, sometimes in the middle of sparring. When you slam pause on your movement as you're pumping with adrenaline, you learn how to get quiet, make things disappear, calm your body. This self-regulation of adrenaline was something that transferred to my police work and helped slow my movements, especially during SWAT calls, in order to navigate situations.

Ninjutsu is the art of war; it's not your average martial arts class, but there is always inner meditation, slowing down, listening, and having a Zen element to your warrior experience: listening to your world, internally checking in with your body, breathing, heart rate, etc. If you become part of the attack, it can't hurt you. The same goes for mental anguish.

Ninjutsu has taught me that whether a physical or a mental threat, identify it, accept it, and get rid of it. When working out your body, it is equally important to connect with your mind. The meditative aspect of martial arts allowed me to become a better person and started me down a path of internal peace.

Maybe eight or nine years after getting into the meditative warrior concept, Greg brought us on a 48-hour woods meditation retreat in northern Pennsylvania. You picked a tree in the woods, Greg drew a circle around it, and you were not to leave the circle except to go to the bathroom. All I had was water…and my thoughts. I thought I knew how to breathe and meditate and quiet my thoughts—I thought I'd been doing that all along—but it was only after the first 24 hours or so, after I had thought about anything and everything, that my mind truly quieted, and I began to deal with my feelings, particularly the death of my father. This experience by myself put cracks in my bubble, and I started getting better from then on.

A few months later, I was on a midnight shift in the dead of winter. It was so peaceful as I sat in my cruiser and looked out over New Haven, when it just hit me: I was pissed that my father had died. I was an absolute mess for a day or two, really letting it sink in that I had been holding onto so much anger at his death. The 48-meditation was the catalyst for this realization, and I finally realized why I'd worked myself to exhaustion for so many years.

I think I've been improving who I am since then. Society's increasing openness to counseling for police and other first responders allowed me to be more open, and if I see something horrible, I deal with it emotionally because everyone gets injured from that exposure, even if you don't realize it at the time. I'm still dealing with stuff but now on a much more open level and can express those emotions more now.

Martial arts was the drug that kept me sane, but, at times, over-training also prevented me from dealing with what I truly had to deal with. It kept me going and was my life saver, but ultimately it was meditation that broke that bubble of anger, and Greg was always there to point me in the right direction. Spiritually, I got better with church when I met my wife, and it brought in that aspect. Faith gives me another source of strength in addition to meditations and the Zen I find through martial arts.

If you don't unearth your mental pain, the physical work you put in won't be as beneficial for processing your actual problems. Workouts kill the pain, but somewhere in there, a system of Zen meditation is the key to unlocking that peace and bringing you back into your own self, your own world, and that's where you ultimately have to be to get growth.

Healing and Connecting with a Love Letter to Self

Kate Deeks
Military Family

Explore the truth of your inner self and prompt universal connection by making "I am" statements releasing illusion."

One way to read the virtue of temperance is living while seeking balance. This activity seeks balance in self-perception through a love letter to oneself. Don't worry, we won't be using poetry.

Writing is hard and writing in the first person is even harder. Many people (including myself) do not enjoy or find it easy to share stories or our true feelings. As a writing coach, when I help people share their experiences or important inner struggles, inevitably I learn about myself as well. In connecting with yourself, you can connect with others. Therefore, we write in spite of the two main reasons people don't like to talk about themselves: the fear of uninformed judgment by others and a belief that actions speak louder than words. Yet there is power in putting thoughts on paper or saying them out loud.

This is an exercise that is simple yet difficult, and I encourage you to do it and not pre-judge what you think it might do.

Calm, Love and Clarity: Letter Activity

Start with a blank page and your favorite pen, or else stand in front of the mirror and speak your responses to your face. Your responses can change your self-perception by stating and understanding what is real and true inside today and releasing half-truths and illusion.

There is no right or wrong way to use this. Do it once to see if it helps. Do it every day to map the edges of your comfort zone. If you find this extremely hard, respond as someone you trust would:

I am safe. Name three ways you are safe right now.

I am loved. Name three ways you are loved right now.

I am listening. Name three ways you are listening right now.

When we have tender emotional/physical/spiritual areas, a way to heal them is by first exploring the edges of the pain/injury/void. No one can tell someone else how to feel. By investigating your own thoughts and feelings today, you make an internal map with the most relevant and "ground-truthed" information. Simple exploration means going to the edge of what is known. When we are an ally to our own healing and put energy into self-discovery the transformation can be immense. Speaking or scribing when feeling hopeless or when wanting to cause harm helps.

By reading this book and investing in your best self, you can become a warrior in a new way: a warrior full of peace and purpose. Discover what needs to heal compassionately from a place of calm, love, and clarity. From here, healing can go forward with the power of self-knowledge.

Do Your Thing

Travis Partington
United States Marine Corps

*Do something that adds value
to others authentically.*

For active military service members, veterans, and non-veterans, I had an idea to create a place to meet and share ideas on how to be there for each other. I looked at different ways to do this and decided the best way to get the message out was to use a podcast/internet radio format. And so, Oscar Mike Radio was born.

To take a step back: 2014 had to be the lowest point in my life. I felt disconnected from friends, family and wanted to shut myself off from life. About that time, I joined the Marine Corps League and started going to funerals of veterans who had committed suicide. I knew I was in a valley in my life but could not figure out why my fellow veterans had abandoned hope and chosen a permanent solution to a temporary problem. I knew I wanted to do something but was not sure what to do. Write a blog? I can write, but wasn't sure if that would work. I could do a video show, but even though I do video now, I passionately believe I have a face for radio.

Right around this time, I started doing guest hosting at WVBF AM 1530 in Taunton, MA. I was on the show "South Shore News and Views", and I had a really great time working on the radio. An idea started to form that I could do a radio show; however, there were several barriers to launching on an AM/FM station. I did not have the money for airtime nor did I have sponsors who could help me pay for the airtime; I also was not able to dedicate to going to a physical location due to work and other obligations.

Some time went by and in April 2016, I went to the first Dale Dorman Media Day at Massasoit Community College. My voice teacher suggested I go and meet with some media professionals, and believe me, that day really changed everything.

More than the voiceover breakout sessions, I wanted to check out the Whoobazoo workshop on podcasting. Whoobazoo is a podcast network run by Keith Hayes and Anthony Arnold. Keith was talking about getting into podcasting and what a podcaster could do if they were willing to apply themselves. I took notes and talked with Keith after the workshop. He asked me what I was going to be podcasting about and asked if I had any audio editing experience. I told him I wanted to do a military/veteran's podcast and I was going to call it Oscar Mike Radio. When Keith asked why, I told him "Oscar Mike" can mean "On the Move" or "On Mission"; I felt that would capture what I was trying to do with the show. Keith told me to download Audacity and a digital audio workstation program and to record something.

With some help, I got a laptop, microphone and started recording. On July 22nd, 2016, my first show dropped. Five people listened to it, and honestly? It was pretty bad. Podcasting is not like being on the radio; because it is recorded, and you are often by yourself—including when you edit your work—my tone, pacing and energy was just not there. But I did it. Keith gave me some advice and candidly told me what to do to improve, and I just kept working, reading, trying, and failing to improve.

Slowly but surely, I started to get in a groove. Preparing for a podcast became easier; I started to relax, and I worked to get in a place where I was driving a 5-Ton in the Marine Corps pulling inert missiles to the range talking with another Marine. This is where the podcast started getting fun and before I knew it, I was at number 100.

Episode 100 was significant because I had (at the time) WAAF DJ Mistress Carrie on my podcast. Having her on helped me in so many ways: a guest like Mistress Carrie demonstrated I could talk to people in a way that was engaging and authentic. I started working to improve my craft when it came to interviews.

It was about this time that I noticed a change in myself and my approach to life. I was not so closed off to people. Even though Oscar Mike Radio does not pay me anything, knowing that I had to outline, produce, and promote content weekly forced me to engage with others in a way that I hadn't done before. I enjoyed the challenge of trying to bring life to a story or a person's struggle to victory on a weekly basis. Having something to do and execute on to the best of my ability got me believing in myself.

I have talked with veterans, Gold Star family members, CEOs, film makers, artists, trauma victims, business owners and coaches, volunteers, heads of nonprofits and people everywhere who support veterans. One of the highlights of 2020 was talking with Kev Breen of Immersive Labs who served in the United Kingdom's Royal Corps of Signals. Getting to share what Kev is doing with Immersive Labs is proof that what I am doing has value. Understanding this has led me to embrace the unknown and say "yes" when saying "no" may have been the safer, less risky option.

As I write this, #220 drops: December 30th, 2020. I am excited for the future. Giving of myself to do this show has provided a purpose and way to learn about myself. I have learned that there is nothing I cannot do. I have learned that asking for help is a good thing. I would tell anyone that you do not have to suffer alone. There are still people out there who are "Oscar Mike" to ensure no one gets left behind.

It may not be a podcast, or a video show, but whatever you are thinking about as "your" thing, I would say do it. Do it with one hundred percent effort and determination, with no expectation of a reward and compensation. I will not promise you fame or fortune, but I will promise that you will change your life and the lives of those around you. This is my Life Hack. Do something that adds value to others authentically, and you will come away healed and restored in a way that a pill will never be able to do. You can do it. I believe in you; just take the first step.

PART III

TACTICS FOR MIND/ BODY SUPPORT

MIND AND BODY tactics are wonderful complements and can be a simple extension to the previous sections on well-being and self-compassion. All the content hacks grouped within *The Resilient Warrior* are bridges linking your mind to your body. The following tactics are simple and profound, activities you may employ to become more mindful, act with purpose, and stimulate your senses.

During the process of writing this book and working closely with the contributors we slowly began introducing some of these tactics into our daily routines throughout the course of the year. We started paying attention more closely to elevated hygiene practices to start looking and feeling good, with the benefits of enhanced health. Disciplines that laid dormant such as Yoga and martial arts were brought back with a newfound enthusiasm and attack. If these two arts have been part of your daily regimen or you're a newbie don't forget the simple things of paying attention, safety, and knowing your own body's physical limitations. Don't be too soft where you deny yourself the push and the benefits. Allow yourself to go all the way, because if you don't why the hell are you attempting it in the first place? The best part is that there are so many options/variations of these physical and mindful arts out there. Use the contributors' inspiration to spark and derive your own practice(s). Innovate the spaces you inhabit to practice your moves and patterns.

The stimulation practices presented within provide an excellent opportunity to eliminate negative energy. The relationship may be auditory or visual. The following content may even challenge your belief systems if you haven't been exposed to such things. We ask that you keep an open mind and give it a go. If you can persevere and make it a regular practice the results can be profound and may even advance your personal story.

Your mission is to act with purpose, become more mindful and stimulate your senses. Go ahead and be kind to yourself—draw a bubble bath, Warrior.

Shaving Comfort & Hygiene

Joe Wadanoli
Master Barber,
United States Coast Guard Auxiliary

Practicing good hygiene is a rewarding, mindful practice that will also help reduce stress and anxiety.

To some people, shaving is no big deal. They wake up, splash some water on the face; a schemer of shave cream and zip-zam-zoom, see ya later! For many others, however, shaving is an intimidating, uncomfortable, downright painful task! Razor nicks, razor bumps, burn, rash, ingrown hairs…the list goes on. All of these are nasty things and when not meticulously kept clean can cause infection. Here are some tactics you can implement into your shave routine that will not only keep you looking and feeling good but also protect your overall health.

Skin preparation. The base to a good shave is preparing the skin, and this is as simple as washing your face! Use warm water with a washcloth and some mild soap. Lightly scrub your face. This will loosen and remove any dead skin, dirt and oil that may be present. This works best while taking a warm shower. Another way to maximize your skin comfort and protection is to apply pre-shave oil. Pre-shave oil can be purchased in different fragrances and essential oils to suit anybody's senses. You also can easily make it yourself by mixing the following in a small container:

3 shot glass castor oil

1 shot glass of olive oil

11 drops lavender essential oil (or any skin safe essential oil)

5 drops Vitamin E oil

To use, add a dime-sized amount of oil into your hand and rub your palms together. Massage it into the desired area. The oil will further the softening of hair and add a layer of lubrication to the skin for your blade to glide smoothly across.

Cutting edge razors. Chances are, you have seen the prices of razors! With an understanding of budget in mind, the adage "You get what you pay for" still reigns supreme. But that does not mean buying a $50+ razor will get you the best shave of your life. The professional opinion is that any double or triple bladed major manufacturer disposable razor will do fine. With that said, you do want to have the *sharpest* razor you can have. The sharper the blade, the easier it cuts the hair, ultimately giving you the most comfort. When you feel the razor pulling, its time to replace the blade. The size of the area that you shave coupled with the coarseness of your hair will determine your own blade's life. For some of us, that means a new blade every shave, but the average rule of thumb is 2 to 3 uses. To help prolong the life of your razor, rinse it clean and shake dry before storing in a dry place.

Shave with the grain. Run your hand down your face. Feels smooth, right? Now run your hand up your face. Kind of like sandpaper, huh? That sandpaper feel is "against the grain". Avoid shaving this direction, it will cut the hair too short and as it grows back it can become ingrown and provide an open vector for bacteria to get inside the pore. This is most prone to be on the neck but can occur anywhere on the body.

Shaving cream. The main purpose of shaving cream is to lubricate the skin for the razor to glide with ease. Find one that has aloe or tea tree oil added, or else try substituting your shave cream with Shea butter, coconut oil, or aloe lotion. It will work just as well (if not better) than the regular stuff. Make sure you rinse off the razor well between strokes!

Start with a quarter to half-dollar sized amount of shave cream, gel or lotion in your palm using your palm as a cup. Then, with the back of your other hand's fingers, apply it to the skin in a circular motion. This will aid in standing the hairs up for a clean cut. You should have a thin layer of lather on your skin, not a full Santa beard of cream—a little goes a long way! Rinse the blade under warm water while tapping the razor head in the sink to knock out any hair caught between the blades. *Never* wipe the hair out of the razor with your finger. You will cut your finger.

After-shave. Traditional aftershaves contain alcohol. Unfortunately, alcohol dries your skin out, which is counterproductive for our purpose. Tea tree oil will help with soreness and redness and protect from infection because tea tree oil contains anti-inflammatory and antimicrobial properties, which make it a perfect post shave option to penetrate the newly open pores and raw skin.

Bumps and acne. If you are prone to razor bumps, press a cold wet washcloth on the bumps after shaving or whenever you feel the need. The cold water will help shrink the bumps down and sooth any discomfort related. Always keep the affected area moisturized. Lots of us also suffer from pimples. A great way to combat acne is to dab a cotton ball with some apple cider vinegar.

The acids in the vinegar will neutralize fungus and bacteria found in acne; it will also help with acne scarring. Apply to the area morning and night; fresh aloe applied to the area has been known to soothe painful acne and help with scaring as well. There are aloe gels and lotions you can purchase or better yet buy an aloe plant. Just cut inch sized ends off the plant and use the fresh aloe from inside. Just do not forget to water the plant!

R and R. Shaving is a violent act we put our skin through. That is why in between shaves, it is vital to nourish your skin with hydration, not only from drinking plenty of water but by applying a moisturizing cream to your skin. Some jobs require a clean shave. If you can get away with it, shave every 2 to 3 days. This will give your skin time to rejuvenate itself. There are certain waivers that can be obtained if your shaving-related skin problems become a doctor-treated medical issue.

If only one thing sticks with you from my advice, let it be this. Do not rush, take your time, smell the fragrances. Make your shave become a favorite part of your routine. Shaving can be a rewarding mindful practice that will also help reduce stress and anxiety. A good shave will leave you feeling invigorated. Shaving is profoundly good for the mind, body, and soul.

Self-Soothing with Bubble Baths

Carol Gee
United States Air Force, veteran caretaker

*Utilize a bubble bath to de-stress
and unwind.*

"Ahh," I sighed as I slid into a bathtub of hot water full of frothy bubbles. Leaning back against the padded rubber bath pillow, I exhaled as the hot water covered my entire body. In my mind's eye, I could still hear the blip, blip, blip, of the various machines hooked up to my husband. The sounds seemed to pulsate throughout my entire body every time they sounded. While under the tangle of tubes and wires and oblivious to everything around him, my husband slept. "Heart attack" the doctor said, walking into the Cardiac Intensive Care Unit with my husband's chart in hand, and asking me how old he was—all seemingly in the same breath.

As I told him his age, I remembered thinking 44 years old seemed way too young for something so serious to have happened. Standing by, I felt helpless: a feeling that I absolutely detested.

The female half of a two-military servicemen couple, both long retired from two successful careers, all my life I've had to use skills honed in the military to resolve problems. For the past 27 years, my husband has battled one chronic health issue after another. Married without children and no immediate family in the area, it has always been just me as his caregiver. Every time I have sat in the 'family' waiting room of a hospital, I have felt much like Alice, tumbling down the rabbit hole, feeling nervous, frightened…alone.

Unknowingly, this same feeling would be repeated over and over, throughout the years. Although each instance (two heart attacks, a small stroke, diabetic foot wounds) initially scared me to death, addressing each in a step-by-step methodical manner has helped me get through all of them. And with each new diagnosis, I would immediately go into warrior mode.

Once we had received the diagnosis, I sought next steps. As my husband is a quiet man, this includes my asking questions—tons of questions—about his care. Are there more tests? Procedures such as hospitalizations, surgery? What about aftercare? What can I do to ensure my husband gets the best prognosis for the future? Focusing on each incident step by step, makes me feel like I have some control, and am part of the solution.

Telling myself to take a deep breath, I force myself to let the hot, sudsy water do its thing. This particular day, I had added a few caps full of *Dr. Teal's Eucalyptus* and *Spearmint Foaming Bath*.

A fanatic of the lovely scents found at *Bath and Body Works*, I often pondered whether I should see about investing in stock in the company. Adding Bath and Body Works Black Raspberry Vanilla to my washcloth, I washed away the fears of that day.

You see, bubble baths have always been my way of dealing with stress. While most folks take showers for a quick refresh (and I typically do so in the mornings), science states that a bubble bath is better for one's mental health than showers. A bubble bath forces you to slow down. Submerging in hot water can also help with pain and inflammation and one's circulation. Lastly, a bubble bath allows you to take a few extra minutes to simply exhale.

For me, turning off the lights, adding a candle, Madagascar Vanilla shower gel, A Thousand Wishes shower gel, or Dark

Kiss Shower Gel, leaves me, my bath water and even the entire bathroom smelling fabulous. Smoothing a body lotion of the same scents afterward, guarantee the scents last long after my bath.

Alas, when people think of men and women serving in the military, or those of us who previously served, they picture someone hard, tough; for example, when folks learn I served, they say, "I wouldn't have thought you were ever in the military. You took too soft, too feminine." (Do they think all servicewomen look like brawny men)? To which I reply that my love of smelling good, and my love of all things pink and girlie, aside, that I am tough. After all, life has demanded that I be. However, even the toughest person you know needs to find a way to promote self-care, to unwind, to decompress. Some find it through working out, through running, through jumping out of parachutes. (Are those folks nuts)? Others find it through painting or some other outlet.

So if bubble baths are your thing, or you think taking them will help you to relax as it does me, you can typically find bubble soap or bath gels at local stores. And while many Bath and Body Works stores in local malls have closed, you can find the above scents and tons of others on their website.

The Air Force changed my whole life's trajectory. It also inspired fearlessness, As such, I'm unafraid of changes. Be it new ideas, (admitting I adore bubble baths), locales, or situations. In my heart, I am still a warrior. Always have been. Always will be.

Colors

Amanda Hudes
Creator of Smiling Through Chaos

Colors are integral to visual stimulation.

I remember living the good life in Manhattan: working, going out dancing a couple of times a week, enjoying my early twenties. Thinking back, I didn't even realize what my close friend was going through.

While I had gone off to college at a fashion school in the city, he had enlisted in the Marines. What different lives we would lead for the next few years; I would check in with him sometimes, and we remained close, but I remember when he came back home after his travels to the Middle East, he would not speak of his time over there. He remained very private, and to this day we still haven't spoken about that time of his life. While I was getting dressed up, he was camouflaging himself into the scenery so he wouldn't be seen.

I cannot say what he went through or is currently going through, or what any of you have gone through, but I can imagine there are definite struggles and challenges. Thank you for your service. Now it's time for *you*.

You are meant to shine. No more hiding. Who are you? What do you want to show to the world? How do you get out of the mindset of, "I need to fit in," regardless of whether that means wearing the same uniform as everyone around you or making sure you are not seen?

Whether you have worn a navy uniform, green, white or any other color, you have been trained to work as a team, to dress the same, to work together, to focus on the work and not on yourselves. You have been conditioned to dress the same, act the same, and do what you are told. Now it's time for you to explore what makes you, *you*! What makes you unique? What makes you stand out?

What you choose to wear each day will affect your mood, your productivity, your attitude towards life! If you are not sure how to start, just get dressed.

Then, answer these questions:

1. What is your favorite color? Quick answer, no thinking about it, just first instinct.

2. What patterns are you most attracted to? Look at animal prints, plaids, gingham, stripes, and abstract patterns, and see what you tend to gravitate towards. It might be that you do not like patterns at all! But that is for *you* to explore.

3. Now try putting a few colors and/or patterns together, next to each other. You can do this in Excel, or you can do it by taking a few shirts and putting them next to each other. Do any get you excited? Do any make you smile, even if only on the inside? Try wearing a red shirt. Look in the mirror. What does it do to your mood? Now try blue. Any change?

What you choose to wear, what you choose to surround yourself with, the color of the walls in your home, the type of people… all of it makes a huge difference in your life. Making sure you have your go-to people to inspire and motivate you each day is also key. Whether you have wonderful relationships with people or visit @SmilingThroughChaos on Instagram, each day to turn your frown upside down, and surround yourself with people who help you focus on the good in this world.

Now, I'm not going to suggest you suddenly become someone who meditates for an hour each day if you are "so not that person." I am not, and I have no shame about it. But do you know what I *have* found to be helpful in calming myself when I start to get anxious? Meditative walks. Take 10 minutes and go for a walk. No talking, just listening. Hear the birds, the leaves blowing in the wind, the cars, just notice each noise until you feel a sense of calm. If the noises are too much for you at first, listen to calm music while walking. Don't push yourself. Do what feels right for *you*.

As you notice yourself laughing more, having more positive thoughts, write them down, what is making you happier. Keep that list next to your bed and look at it, one, two, three times a day, and focus on the good. Celebrate *life*.

Stimulation

Sumuer Watkins

Finding the right music is key to stimulating a sense of calm and well-being.

Every action in your body is deliberate. You may not be conscious of it, but it *is* deliberate. Information is sent from the brain to other parts of the body through messages disguised as electrical impulses. These messages give specific commands and return specific responses to the stimuli.

One of the primary routes for these messages to travel is through the vagus nerve, which is the longest and most complex, nerve in your body. As such, it communicates information with nearly every organ. Naturally, if the vagus nerve is working at less-than-optimal levels, we would expect to find ourselves feeling less than optimal.

Stimulation of the vagus nerve has proven to be effective for the treatment of a myriad of ailments including depression, anxiety, epilepsy, and Alzheimer's disease. Even the FDA has recognized stimulation of the vagus nerve as a valid form of treatment to minimize the symptoms of depression and epilepsy in severe cases. Finding music that stimulates the vagus nerve can significantly increase our feeling of well-being and minimize anxiety. Research indicates that music can have a positive effect on one's perception of life's situations. For example, a randomized clinical trial showed that music therapy significantly decreased anxiety.

However, not all music is helpful for our mental health. Some music can leave us feeling agitated and anxious just as quickly as other music leaves us calm or joyful. Finding the right music is key. Meditation music can be especially calming.

Many listeners attest to music set to 432hz or 528hz to be healing in nature by reducing anxiety, elevating mood, and decreasing blood pressure. A simple search on any music streaming platform for 432hz or 528hz will offer countless musical options. Some find listening to this type of music while sleeping allows them to wake up refreshed and looking forward to the day. Because the music can cause your body to release toxins, it is important to drink plenty of water after listening to the healing music to help wash the toxins out.

Bilateral Stimulation for Trauma with Pickup Basketball

Rich Walton
"Box and One" Basketball

Incorporate bilateral stimulation to aid and assist with trauma, while restoring positive energy.

Every now and again, we all must face something that bothers us. Oftentimes, it can be circumstantial (such as bad news), or information that is just upsetting, or we are just having a bad day for any number of reasons.

When people are dealing with some sort of trauma that is really bothering them, they tend to get deep in thought, and exhibit these 1,000 miles "death stares;" just staring off into an abyss, ruminating and fixating on the one thing that is bothering them.

The truth is, we need movement to move thoughts and alleviate stress.

Back in 1987, while walking in a park, Dr. Francine Shapiro noticed that when she moved her eyes side to side, some upsetting thoughts and feelings that she had suddenly disappeared. Her simple eye movement discoveries led to incredible breakthroughs in treating people for PTSD.

The treatment is called Eye Movement Desensitization Reprocessing, or EMDR. And it is all based on *one thing*: bilateral stimulation.

So, what can you do to help yourself feel good, deal with your life's challenges and stresses, and get out of your own head?

You guessed it.

Bilateral stimulation with basketball. Bilateral stimulation with a basketball creates positive energy and helps bring about so many positive feelings. Next time something is bothering you, instead of staring off into space, just try moving your eyes side to side for a minute or two. Maybe even pickup basketball and shoot 50 free throws.

Odds are, you will probably feel a little better. Better yet, there is a real scientific reason for it. Our brains are one of the most complex things in all of the universe. Deep inside of our brains we have something called the "Corpus Callosum," which is what allows information to pass through *both* sides of our brain. When it is active, both sides of our brains communicate.

Pretty cool stuff, right? So take advantage of it: keep working on your bilateral movement and bilateral stimulation to keep feeling good, healthy, happy, and strong.

Mindful Meditation

Maverick Willet
United States Army, Ranger

Receive mental clarity, mindfulness, and health benefits from taking cold showers.

The crucial component of maintaining my mental health and focus has been my morning regimen of a cold shower upon waking followed by mindful meditation.

The cold shower is a daily step into discomfort. Aside from the metabolic benefits, it is an exercise of mental fortitude to do something my body is resisting. I also gain a lot of mental clarity from the practice.

With meditation, I can tap into my authentic self, the part of me that does not live in a conditioned state of stress, doubt, fear, approval, or worry. Through this practice I can be present and practice active gratitude for all that I have. In practicing gratitude, I make room for more abundance in my health, wealth, and relationships. As a veteran and entrepreneur, this daily ritual helps me remain intuitive, resourceful, and open-minded to new methods of business growth. I am also able to be authentic in my content for viewers and clients, as well as be fully present with my wife and son.

In this world of constant negativity, this combination of a simple cold shower and mindful meditation has been the most effective practice to remain positive and focused on my personal development and thrive despite a tumultuous economic/political climate. I have realized that one becomes what is habitually consumed, so I strive every day to consume things that bring value to my life. I limit who I follow on social media, as to only expose myself to people who add to my current mission of self-improvement and business growth.

You can only grow and prosper whilst living as your authentic self. Our conditioned minds operate on fear and approval and stagnate us. It keeps us from taking risks or stepping outside of our comfort zone. However, you cannot fix what you do not know, and most people don't even realize they live this way. Mindful meditation is a great tool to become aware of these thoughts and break patterns in your life that are keeping you from being your best self.

Mindful Marksmanship

Ben King & Joe Hamilton
United States Army

Make "Mindful Marksmanship" a hobby to help enhance psychological and emotional control.

The Warrior Life Hack they teach and use to help maintain their mental health is a mindfulness meditation practice modeled after military marksmanship training. Over the last two years, even during the pandemic, they have trained veterans all over the world how to hack their mental health and marksmanship ability teaching attention as the ultimate variable for both.

Since the invention of the rifle, the military has taught the necessary physical components of being a marksman. Things like breath control, posture, alignment positioning, etc. are primarily "physically" oriented.

However, as many world class performers (both competitive and combat experienced) can attest, mental focus is crucial to high-level shooting performance. Unfortunately, teaching the psychological component of shooting performance is an area where the military has historically fallen short. Specifically, many service members have been left to "figure it out" on their own and are unaware of specific tools or actions that can improve their focus and subsequently their performance. In short, the physical or technical part of shooting is relatively straightforward and not what separates high and low performers.

Therefore, what we suggest in the Mindful Marksmanship program is that what is needed to take a marksman to the highest level is, in fact, psychological and emotional control. Mindfulness practice has proven to be one of the most effective tools at developing exactly the type of psychological and emotional control that is critical to shooting performance. The Mindful Marksmanship program leverages current research, best practices, and expertise from both the mindfulness and tactical training communities.

Mindfulness. It is *your* attention. Your attention can be trained. It is the most foundational component of your consciousness and mental health.

Marksmanship. You miss because of misplaced attention or subconscious errors. Extreme focus is required for extreme performance. Mindfulness is the best tool in the toolbox to train your focus shooting.

There is a perfect symbiotic relationship between marksmanship and mindfulness. With proper framing, one is good for training the other and is evidenced by improvements in both.

The quick and dirty on accurate shooting. Any decent firearms instructor can teach people how to stand, grip/hold the gun, and align the sights in about 10 minutes. This is evidenced through "dry fire," "snapping in" or conducting a "dime drill." But why is it that we can teach this in 10 minutes, and everyone can do it perfectly…but then they can't hit the target? The problem is that in all of those drills, the gun is not loaded and they know it. Therefore, the anxiety associated from the shot, whether it be from anticipation of recoil and muzzle blast or anxiety related to performance, the anxiety is not there. Despite useless pie charts you may have seen indicating that you are "heeling, pushing, jerking, thumbing, flinching, etc." the truth is it doesn't matter: the problem and solution are even more straightforward. What *is* going on every time you miss (assuming the gun is zeroed, and the sights are aligned) is that the gun was moved during the final portion of the firing process (pressing the trigger).

The key here is that this error is almost always done sub-consciously and therefore is more difficult to overcome than simply stating repeatedly "stop jerking the trigger." This undesir-able response can only be overcome through deliberate practice and conditioning. This type of deliberate practice requires more cognitive horsepower and energy than folks are used to applying. But it doesn't take as long as you might think. The tools and skills used in mindfulness meditation are identical to the skills needed to execute marksmanship performance on demand.

Mindfulness fundamentals. Put simply, *mindfulness* refers to our ability to pay attention, particularly in the *present* moment. Despite popular beliefs like "I can't pay attention" or "I'm just a scatterbrained person" because of this or that, your attention is not an innate or fixed asset. Think of your attention as more like a muscle and less like bone structure. In other words, you can train your attention. Mindfulness is attention—it can be changed, it is a lot more important than you think and it is the key that opens all the doors. Your attention and how you regulate your attention is the prism through which all your behaviors filter through. Mindfulness is a hack against the behaviors that we do not want to do but often feel like we cannot control.

The key to basic mental management is your ability to pay attention to what is happening in your own mind. If you are not aware of what is going inside your body and mind, then there is never going to be anything you are going to be able to do about it. In marksmanship terms, mindfulness is the trigger press. A quick internet search will let you know that mindfulness has been shown to significantly reduce stress, increase emotional intelligence and self-compassion, we don't have the real estate to go into exhaustive detail about the benefits here, but rest assured this practice is worth your time.

Bringing the two together (theoretically) making the connection through practical exercises.

Practical Exercise I: "Tame the Mind, Train the Mind"

Next time you find yourself caught up in a story, or ruminating on a stress-inducing environment, use your senses to bring your mind into the present moment and use the alignment of your posture to train your mind to stay focused on your body instead of focused on the story being created in your mind.

Step 1. Curiosity tames the mind every time. Because so much of our thinking is narrating a story, use the mind's own proclivities to create quieter. In the world of mindfulness meditation this technique is called mantra. Here is how you do it to tame your mind. Ask your mind what information from your senses are most noticeable. It may sound funny, but literally say in your head: 'OK, mind, what do you see? What do you hear? What do you feel?' As a warrior, you are probably familiar with situational awareness so just put your mind in that mindset and study the present moment with your senses.

Step 2. Connect to your body by breaking it into six chunks and systematically assess your body for comfort and upright posture. Again, narrate in your mind: 'OK, mind, what do you feel at your feet? What do you feel at your hips, what do you feel at your core, what do you feel at your heart space, what do you feel at your head space?'

Step 3. Lastly, after you have created an upright and alert posture, put a little smile on your face.

Practical Exercise II: Process-Focused Anxiety Inoculation Drill

On the range, one of the best drills we have found to improve accuracy is by combining the use of a "script" or "mantra", a common mindfulness technique with the classic marksmanship "ball and dummy" drill. It is best done as a two-person drill but can be done solo by using "dummy rounds" or non-firing ammunition. The key to this drill is that the shooter cannot be aware of whether the weapon is loaded or unloaded during the trigger press. This is a process-focused drill and although they are aiming at a target (preferably a difficult one, i.e., one which is small or far away), the point is not whether they hit the target or not. The point is that when they press the trigger and expect the gun to be loaded the front sight (or tip of the barrel) does not move *at all*.

Step 1. The shooter places the weapon on the ground or table and then looks away so that he or she cannot see what their partner is doing. The partner will then either load or unload the weapon (their choice) and place the weapon back on the ground or table. The shooter then picks the weapon up and attempts to place a well-aimed shot at the target. Repeat this step a few times with some live and some dry.

Step 2. The shooter places the weapon on the ground or table and then looks away so that he or she cannot see what their partner is doing. The partner will then either load or unload the weapon (their choice) and place the weapon back on the ground or table. The shooter then brings the weapon into the firing position and the partner goes through a script of questions to focus the shooter's attention. An example would be, if at any point the shooter cannot answer to the affirmative, then the script should be repeated from the beginning. Once the shooter has answered to the affirmative, the final step is the shooter taking all the perceived "slack" out of the trigger system so that the weapons will fire with *any* additional movement. At that point the shooter should *hold* and conduct a LIDDS assessment to scan for anxiety present anywhere in the body. The shooter should then either press the trigger (if they are relaxed and fully in control) or start the process over (if they are anxious or feel like they will flinch). Repeat as many times as necessary until the shooter can pick up the gun and press the trigger without moving the gun whether it is loaded or not.

In both of these drills, the ultimate variable is attention. In marksmanship, we reliably create a stress-inducing experience, which is why using marksmanship is a great tool for training attention. Shifting the value of your marksmanship skills to mindfulness meditation means applying the ultimate variable, *your attention*, to the experience of stress in your daily life.

Purposeful Movement

Dr. Kate Hendricks Thomas
United States Marine Corps

Mindful movement creates opportunities for mastery, experience, and a platform from which to build physical stability.

When we talk about caring for our physical body, we often emphasize movement, movement, off-the-couch movement! Yet balance is one of the most important things a person can plan into a training calendar.

The physical practices that offer us stress reduction and a return to homeostatic balance are beneficial in a myriad of ways. It cannot all be about raising our heart rate and shrinking a derriere. Those things are fine, but balanced physical self-care with a keen focus on regulating an overstimulated nervous system must become priorities to anyone looking to cultivate resilience.

Here is the good news—there is more than one way to do this. You have the freedom to figure out which activities work best for your personality, resources, and preferences. Trying out mindful movement practices and learning from the pros who teach them is my favorite hobby. For me, the most relaxing physical practice available changes based on what is happening in my life. There have been times when the answer was trail running, yoga, swimming, or rowing. The fun part is trying new options out with an eye towards what you should be feeling, and if it is a practice that is bringing you into balance. Remember: healthy practices are not abusive. When it is a balancing activity, you will feel yourself exerting but still peaceful. You will sleep a bit better; you may notice your mind slow down a bit.

You'll pay attention to your body in new ways. *'Hey!'* you'll think. *'I just noticed how much tighter my left hip is than my right! I wonder if I should spend some time stretching that side more?'* Self-care of this sort also provides a level of mental fitness training that can hone focus, improve performance, and increase resilience. Such training involves purposeful movement that brings attentive focus to the physical body and the racing mind. This attention trains the body in both a challenging and balanced fashion while carving in space for activation of the parasympathetic nervous system. It is here that the body restores, improves, and evens out hormone levels in the blood back to their optimal levels. That's the beauty of balanced training: it pushes your envelope and then hits the reset button!

Mindful movement is a unique way to build mental toughness. It creates opportunities for mastery, experience, and a platform from which to build physical stability. Interestingly, most of us are not physically stable without very intentionally working to become so. We sit too much, slouch a bit, and create muscular imbalances that we do not notice because we often zip through our days without paying attention to present-tense sensations in our tissues.

We all live in an obesogenic environment where it is easier to find fast food than fresh vegetables, and we are all constantly overstimulated. It is easy to dismiss just how stimulating our environments typically are because we get used to an unhealthy norm. That cell phone is really not supposed to be next to your pillow at night.

I recall sitting with a friend in a shopping mall a few years ago. We sat down at a little table near the food court and were trying to chat and catch up a bit while she snuggled her toddler in her lap. We were surrounded by flat-screen televisions that were all blaring different stations to entertain food court patrons. Her little boy looked around in alarm, then buried his face in her shoulder and started weeping.

I felt like joining him. His young system was not used to blaring techno-noise and his reaction to the shrillness was to retreat to his mom. I remember thinking that he was setting an example for the adults in the room who had all gotten used to ten television sets blaring overhead while they ate a rushed meal of fast food. This is not normal for our physical bodies!

The pace of modern life is frenetic. Our bodies read this "Go, go, go" message clearly, and the stress embeds itself in our minds and bodies. Our stress response is a completely natural phenomenon, and the human body operates intelligently to produce appropriate reactions to life's surprises. Upon registering some sort of threat, the brain sends hormonal signals to the adrenal glands, which secrete cortisol and adrenaline to empower the body to handle it. In a healthy negative feedback system, the cortisol signals the hypothalamus to shut down the response provided the threat has disappeared. This stress response is supposed to happen at an intensity level in relation to the threat. It is instructive and animal, and is necessary for performance, self-preservation, and survival.

Everyone's response to stimuli differs, and what is stimulating to one person biochemically may not be to another. That does not mean our systems *aren't* registering the stimulation, however. Those ten televisions were keeping my nervous system on the alert, even if I did not view them as threatening in the same way that my friend's toddler did.

The problem with the human stress response does not become apparent until the stress becomes chronic, and the bloodstream contains too much cortisol. Chronic stress occurs when the brain's hypothalamus refuses to shut off the chemical signals it is sending because it still perceives a problem. In our modern society with its constantly ringing phones, troubled interpersonal relationships, and an ever-increasing pace enabled by technology, chronic stress is rampant.

When the body's stress response is constantly firing, blood cortisol levels are too high and inflammatory proteins become more present in the bloodstream. A host of illnesses and inflammatory conditions have been related to this chemical imbalance. The body's immune system becomes overactive and confused by the aberrant proteins. Unsure what foreign bodies to attack, autoimmune illnesses like rheumatoid arthritis and allergies become real health issues. Unchecked, unacknowledged stress is a killer in too many ways to count. Chronic stress has been linked to a host of physical maladies including abdominal weight gain, cancer, gastrointestinal illnesses, depression, and chronic pain.

We cannot always prevent surprises that send our bodies into reaction mode, but we can prepare them for stress and adopt a positive outlook towards challenge, in general. For me, time spent with my pet, a quiet walk in the woods, or a mindful yoga class are my means of preparing for the stress I know will always come.

Consistency Through Yoga

Heather Clark
United States Navy

Incorporate yoga into your lifestyle for sound mind and body.

Consistency in practice of anything is the key element to it becoming habitual. (Keep in mind this applies to negative habits as well.) Being cognizant of this fact is crucial to being able to control your mindset.

Routine is not only a familiar behavior embedded within veterans, but it is an effective method for keeping you on track and accountable. Sticking to what you are already familiar with will make it significantly easier to achieve success. That success is also subjective and relative to each individual. You do not need to be a rock star right away; Leveling up doesn't mean having to reach the top immediately if you are continuing to put into practice regimens that will get you to the next level until you reach the larger goal.

There are multiple elements that contribute to the overall health of a veteran. While I have found yoga to be an effective treatment supplement to physical and mental disabilities, I also realize that there are other areas that need attention. Transitioning successfully into civilian life, for example, requires more than just getting a job. The best life hack as a veteran comes from the knowledge that you need to fulfill multiple needs to transition into civilian life and thrive.

There are eight elements that veterans need to either have in place before they get out or find if they have already left service. These eight elements are like the eightfold path in yoga, which serve as a set of guidelines for living your best life. I use this holistic veteran path in my own life to ensure that I stay healthy, motivated, and moving forward. Acknowledgement and incorporation of these in veteran lives can serve as a guide in their own goals of recovery and success. For this discussion, we will focus on mindfulness, specifically using the tools of yoga, meditation, and mindset.

Course of action. Set up your routine, one which is specifically tailored to you. While there are many guidelines to how you should be doing something, each person is different in their schedules, motivations, and capabilities. For example, using the SMART metric, you can set up realistic goals that will keep you focused and accountable. SMART goal setting means setting goals that are Specific, Measurable, Accountable, Realistic, and Timely.

Magic hour. The ancient practice of Ayurveda was created close to the time that yoga came into practice. Its focus was mainly on diet, but also included insightful information about different body types and their sleep cycles and the best hours of the day to create. An example of this is my own body type or constitution of Kappa, which requires 6 to 8 hours of sleep. My magic hour for waking up is 5:00 am. If I wake up at 4:45 am, I feel groggy all day. If I sleep until 6:00 am, then I feel rushed all day. Hitting the magic hour is the first thing that can make or break your day.

Meditation and mindset. Meditation and positive mindset allow for two things to happen: access to more thoughts and the ability to hold onto a positive thought long enough so it can create an entire new neural circuit. Throw away the notion that you must clear your mind during meditation and instead let your mind go where it needs to go. With your eyes open, the optic nerve only allows for one thing to be processed at time; by closing your eyes during meditation, you have access to more thoughts. By not forcing the "clear your head concept," you can filter through and have access to more information that may be beneficial to you.

At some point, you do need to take the wheel when negative thoughts come. Using methods practiced in cognitive behavior therapy, you can change those negatives to positives. Trauma may rewire your brain, but you can rewire it back. Just like you can create new neural circuits when learning to play an instrument, you can create new circuits of positive thought. The zero-level theorem describes how thoughts have mass, which means that gravity can act upon them. That means they can be controlled. It only takes 17 seconds for a new thought to attach itself and 68 seconds to create an entire new circuit.

Yoga and Pranayama. Yoga is a moving meditation. Combined with pranayama/breathing, certain yoga poses can access parts of your nervous system that get damaged in combat. These poses focus on your hip area where tension and emotion build up, much like they do in your shoulder areas. Breathing with these poses triggers the vagus nerve, which increases neurotransmitter activity, which in turn tells your brain to calm down.

Trauma also can alter your memory processing and cause more emotion to be attached to memories, which is often why memories of combat can be overwhelming. Using correct breathing techniques, you change your memory back to its correct operating system. Adding one last ingredient of sound can speed the process of healing: the sound of Om resonates at the same frequency as nature, and the mudra or hand gesture used in meditation (the thumb to the index finger) sends a signal to your brain to relax. Focus on the fundamentals of both and you will in time make that brain body connection. Both will come naturally to you and you will start to feel the benefits.

Holistic practices like yoga and meditation are things veterans have already been doing since boot camp. Approximately 80 percent of the dynamic and static exercises in military physical training are yoga poses, and techniques like box breathing and mindset are taught in most branches. Putting away Westernized preconceptions of yoga allows us to see it for what it really is: another tool that will increase your mental edge, help with injuries acquired during service and make you into an elite warrior.

Using the technique of Vetspeak, I have tailored military wellness programs created using military culture, yoga, and cutting-edge science. These programs use fitness knowledge that veterans already are familiar with, are choreographed in a way that implements trauma yoga without even realizing it.

Swimming for Health

Jeffrey Miller
United States Army

Harness the "low-impact" style of swimming exercise to assist with injuries, and ultimately mix up your physical fitness routine.

After 28 years of Army mandatory fitness, and even 7 years of grade school and high school sports before that, I finally made the decision that I am sure others with similar backgrounds do: I decided that I had earned the right to *stop* working out. Partly it was because I was no longer expected to do it for the Army, but the truth is that it was not fun, and I was not motivated to change that fact.

Fast forward two and a half years and one doctor visit later, and it was clear a change needed to be made. I had been "planning on going to the gym" for months and months but found no motivation to do it. It wasn't until after receiving my dirty bill of health from my doctor and some encouragement from my kids and friends that I decided it was time to make a change. I went to the local YMCA and signed up. Why the YMCA?

Because it had a pool.

I have always loved swimming and owing to some back and knee issues I developed in the Army, it being a low impact form of exercise made it my best option. I started out slow, only spending about 30 minutes swimming with lots of breaks for rest. The thing I figured out for me was it was not hard to push my limits with swimming. After having goals of making it 200 meters without stopping, it quickly moved to 400, then 600. After only a week of swimming 3 days a week, I was up to 800 meters with only one or two 30-second breaks. This was an instant motivator for me; I felt like I was making massive gains in my endurance and with it being low impact, I did not have the after pains that I expected.

This is when I started to turn back into the Army guy who'd left me for greener pastures a few years ago. I began to demand more of myself, and to maintain my dedication for getting in shape I told everyone at work what I was doing. These were people who would not only listen but would ask me how I was doing periodically. I also told my friends and family, and while I wasn't going to let them down, mostly I needed this for myself.

Currently, I am swimming 1,600 meters per session without stopping. I do not touch the bottom of the pool or push off the wall, so I have the feeling of truly swimming with no break. I am limited on my time in the pool (60 minutes per session), so I am trying to develop different training strategies to increase my workout. While in an Infantry unit, we would conduct water survival training; swimming while wearing your field uniform is quite challenging as it adds drag to your swim, so I will be incorporating this theory by wearing a long-sleeved shirt. I have also ordered a weight belt to add resistance.

Since I have started swimming, not only have I lost a substantial amount of weight, but my energy levels have also been soaring. I am more active during work and after, and I feel more positive about my direction in life. I look forward to going to the gym and plan to add other activities back into my life. Keeping physically fit is invaluable in maintaining mental fitness.

Mental & Physical Health Connection

Ryan Shannon
United States Navy

Do not let life's obstacles/setbacks get in your way; take control of your own physical and emotional health.

Towards the end of my service, I became partially paralyzed during a training accident. I had been diagnosed with PTSD due to multiple experiences, including combatting a fire onboard a submarine in dry-dock that resulted in the total loss of the submarine, a fellow shipmate completed suicide where I was a responder on scene, and the loss of life of other shipmates during my time serving. All these things affected my mental health, and I was not prepared to combat my own spiral into depression and ultimately suicidal ideation.

The physical injury ended my military career, and the subsequent mental health side effects associated with it all came to a point where my brain tricked me into thinking the solution to end this pain was to take my own life and alleviate my family of the "burden" I believed I was. While this is my story, it is not uncommon, which is why I believe what I do is important.

So how did I go from literally minutes away from taking my own life to here? The answer is not extremely complicated, but it also is not easy to do. These are my life hacks.

The first thing I did was take control of my physical health. The last time I'd left the doctor's office was in a wheelchair, unable to walk due to ligament and nerve damage in my left foot with a diagnosis of incomplete paralysis and something called Complex Regional Pain Syndrome (CRPS), which is a rare nerve condition that makes the brain function as if an injury is present even when there is no injury. Basically, to this day, my brain still sends pain signals, swelling and discoloration to my foot as if it were still broken. I started to take back control by getting out of that wheelchair, rehabbing my foot with the aid of a prosthetic device that acts like a cast, going to physical therapy and making sure I took slow lengthy walks every single opportunity I had. Once I became more confident in my ability to walk steadily, I ditched the wheelchair and crutches, and while I still require the prosthetic, I can walk under my own power now.

Not only did I relearn to walk, but I also started jogging, then running, then finding sports that accommodated someone who requires a prosthetic, known as adaptive sports. I eventually went on to compete in the Department of Defense's Warrior Games twice, won four medals in track there, competed at the international level in Prince Harry's Invictus Games where I got a silver medal in track competing against the world's top wounded veterans and eventually started training for the Paralympics with the USA Seated Volleyball team. While this helped me take back my physical health, it was also helping my mental health. I found purpose again in those sports, I was proud of my accomplishments and my family got to witness me physically take my life back.

This was a good start, but I felt that I had more to offer and that's where advocacy comes in. During my physical rehab, music played an important role for me. I decided that I could help other veterans with my story, coupled with music, and I started a non-profit to help facilitate that. We offered free musical instruments, training and events, intended to serve as catalysts to get veterans talking more openly about their mental health. The non-profit eventually failed; I had no idea what I was doing or how to lead an organization.

With that failure in my back pocket, I went back to school and got my MBA. During my time with the nonprofit I started, I networked with a lot of other non-profits working in the mental health space, one of those being Hope for the Day. After I educated myself, I was ready to give the non-profit thing another shot and reached out to Hope for the Day, where we spent two years developing what would become Project R.E.D. Team—the organization's active duty, veteran, first responder and associated families branch within the organization. I now had a platform with massive infrastructure to tell my story, educate people in that community and provide a space where we can start tearing down the stigmas associated with talking about our mental health.

By telling my story over and over, I was finding more and more ways to heal and combat my bad days. I was helping others connect with their own mental health issues and seeing them come forward and discuss their issues. People were no longer "suffering in silence" because we had created a place where openly talking about these things was not taboo or demeaning. I quickly realized that the struggles I went through, the things I did not understand, and the darkest days of my life had become ammo to help others. By being open and honest, I was no longer going to therapy appointments, my VA appointments quickly started becoming non-existent and I was feeling "normal" again. While I do advocate for therapy and going to the doctor, for me this was my new means of therapy. This for me became the ultimate life hack: I was able to sleep better, my relationships improved, I had purpose again, and I created a space to help others in similar positions.

This is why every story matters. This is why I say you do not need to suffer in silence. The more we make talking about these things "the norm," the more we can create a tangible impact and see a reduction in the suicide numbers that plague our community.

"With Steel We Lead"

Carol Welte Richmond,
interviewing her father
Herbert D. (Bud) Welte
United States Army

A successful, fulfilled life thrives on loyal consistency.

If you stop and think about it, it seems obvious anyone who lives to be 88, still living independently, managing the everyday nicely on the family farm has mastered some consistent habits that contribute to well-being.

Bud Welte was an industrial arts teacher in 1956 in Connecticut, and was in his early twenties when he was drafted by the U.S. Army. He served two years with the 534th Field Artillery Battalion, stationed on a former WWII base outside Bad Kissingen, Germany, shipped overseas in December '56 with thousands of other young men. 'With Steel We Lead', it says on a pin he still possesses from that time.

The memories spill out of his mouth slowly as he thinks about it. Numbers might not be as accurate as he'd like, but the names of people he served with and ships he sailed, he remembers. He was the supply clerk for his unit, taking care weekly of each man's laundry, sheets, the like, transporting bags with 4-digit identification numbers every week to Wurtsburg for cleaning, returning the next day for retrieval. "I was Radar O'Reilly," he has said, in reference to a character from the 70's TV show, *M*A*S*H*.

"Was it as much fun as that?" I asked him.

"No," he responded. It wasn't fun. Take home pay was $52 a month. "Subsistence pay, actually. Just basic," he says. A carton of cigarettes was a buck at the post exchange on base. "The first year I taught at Plainville, I got $1500."

The devotion to his family runs deep. The wood working skills he possesses have led him to create a gun cabinet of store quality for each son and grandson, a blanket chest for each daughter and granddaughter.

He walks early every morning after a breakfast he makes himself like a short order cook, if the faithfully frigid winter temps don't intervene. Black lab Lucky and golden retriever Rowdy would remind him if he didn't get his coat on in time. There's a whistling post he and his wife set up on the corner of what's called the south quarter, the land that connects to the yard, and a path through the planted native grasses is mowed in spring and summer and remains adequately accessible once the snow flies. He doesn't think too much about current society-speak, and words like 'self-care' lend to a deer-in-the-headlights return gaze at his interviewer. He doesn't really think about it. He just lives it.

Hiking

Andrew Farrer,
United States Marine Corps & Combat Veteran
Irreverent Warriors District Commander,
Department of Tennessee

Introduce hiking into your lifestyle for improved physical, mental health, and take the opportunity for socialization.

Hiking in its simplest form is the activity of going on long walks. Those long walks usually consist of navigating local nature trails or the varied terrain such as forests, deserts, and mountains. Hiking in groups takes individuals out of their isolation. Hiking gets you out in nature, breathing the fresh air, and experiencing the elements. When you bring a pack with snacks and water, you are adding some extras and engaging your body in a multitude of physical exercise.

The action of hiking is also a great self-care tool for making you more accountable to yourself. The action provides you with some of the best coping strategies and mindfulness to help combat your specific ailments and suffering.

The benefits are many, including:

1.   An outlet for healthy and compassionate relationships.

2. A mender of emotional wounds and a healer for physical wounds.

3. Engages your body with cardiovascular exercise (exercise that engages your heart rate).

4. Engages your body in hand, eye coordination and balance (with foot and hand placement).

5. Strengthens core muscles.

6. Strengthens legs, bones, and muscles throughout the body.

7. Improves overall mental health (void of distractions/technology and a boost to overall mood by lowering anxiety and stress and increasing dopamine levels).

The more you hike, the more you start to improve and when you hike with others there is an accountability piece to keep on moving and improving, as well as the desire to try more difficult hikes with varied terrain.

Irreverent Warriors, a nationwide organization helping veterans, uses the comfort of "silkies"—known to the military community as the PT (physical training) silk shorts. Silkies are used by the military when they work out and Irreverent Warriors has embraced that as the uniform of choice when they go on their hikes. Silkies are an old military tradition that has been eliminated by the military and one which they have chosen to revive because of the nostalgia and the laughter that they create.

Hiking in combat boots and carrying a ruck has been an important part of military culture and training since the beginning of time. Combat and non-combat veterans alike enjoy the camaraderie created during shared misery. The laughter and the sense of purpose remind us that the brotherhood and camaraderie that they once had in the military will never die and they will always be there for each other.

Bringing veterans together through humor and camaraderie improves their quality of life. Be that through the Silkies Hikes, or other events—BBQ's, sporting/music events, family picnics, happy hours, reunions, or simply getting together in someone's living room.

The end result is fewer veterans who kill themselves.

The Outdoors

Dr. Byron Davis
United States Marine Corps

Experience the outdoors and use it as a source for enhanced well-being.

Dr. Byron Davis is a Marine Corps veteran (2008–2013) and current narcotics K-9 officer in middle Tennessee (2014–present). As a Marine, Dr. Davis witnessed the struggles of fellow unitary Marines because of their overseas service in campaigns such as Operation Enduring Freedom and Operation Iraqi Freedom. It was during this time that he realized the significance of post-traumatic stress disorder and just how misunderstood the disorder was among his fellow warriors. As a result, he began his journey toward obtaining his doctoral degree with his focus in the field of psychology with the hopes of developing unique approaches to alleviating PTSD symptoms.

While working in Afghanistan as a security contractor, Dr. Davis reflected on his own past and how he utilized Mother Nature to combat stress prior to joining the Marine Corps. It was during this period of reminiscence where the idea of Dogs of War Outdoors was created. In 2016, Dr. Davis followed through with that idea and created the organization. In 2018, after gaining traction among fellow warriors across all branches of service, he created the Dogs of War Foundation. Since the creation, the organization has taken many warriors on outdoor adventures such as hunting, fishing, hiking, and camping trips to help combat PTSD.

Mother Nature provides both serenity and calmness with no side effects. In an age where medical providers attempt to suppress our struggles with narcotics, it is essential that we explore the other various avenues available to help us cope. Over the course of many years, Dr. Davis developed a theory relevant to suicide among our nation's warriors.

There are three things that we need to push forward with our lives:

Camaraderie. When we enter the military, we create indestructible bonds. We maintain a willingness to sacrifice our own lives for our fellow warrior and they will do the same for us. That just isn't something that is common in society. When we exit the military, we lose that camaraderie and therefore lose a piece of our soul.

Comfort. While surrounded by fellow warriors, we all know they have our back. We are not required to consistently search for threats and struggle with the thought of falling prey to a hunter like ourselves. We can relax because we know we're safe.

Adrenaline. We are trained to kill while in the military and there is no other adrenaline that parallels a hunt for human beings. But it isn't necessarily the hunt for human beings that provides the adrenaline. It's just the hunt. It's that familiar feeling of being a predator once again. We do not need ample amounts of adrenaline. We need just enough to satisfy our desire to do exactly what we're trained to do.

Regardless of the activity, being surrounded by nature helps us relax. When we're on a hunting, fishing, camping, or hiking trip, we allow ourselves to observe other living creatures carrying out their lives surrounded by only the sounds of nature. Being in the outdoors and knowing that we're safe and secure presents a level of tranquility that cannot be matched elsewhere. Undesirable noise pollution isn't present; only the desirable and calming sounds of the wilderness, such as the wind blowing through the canopy. The air is fresh, and the water is pure. We aren't consistently looking over our shoulder in search of threats. Our attention is focused on the living creatures around us, which have very few responsibilities outside of just survival, and we can relate. We share commonalities. For many of us, our only goal at that point in our lives is just survival. For a moment, we don't feel as though we are a burden on others, and we have a desire to live. Mother Nature does not offer criticism and as a result, we can think through our struggles without fear of judgement or repercussion.

We aren't broken or abnormal. Rather, we are just a different type of normal. We are the result of an evolutionary mindset and have been molded into a warrior. From a biological perspective, we look no different than others. However, our minds operate differently. We are both prepared for and maintain an expectation of violence each day, which most wouldn't understand. It is my belief that our traditional means of psychological treatment is less effective on our veteran population. Yet, mainstream psychological agendas consistently utilize these approaches and often fail. An exploration of alternative treatment options is crucial, especially considering veteran suicide remains a significant issue. Currently, there are many organizations in America that dedicate their time and service to the protection of our nation's veterans.

Making Realistic Changes

Becky Hanna, RN
Veterans' Advocate

Make the appropriate changes to seek improvement. Make sure your goals are actionable, specific, and measurable.

What is most important to you today, in your life? How do you want to live your best warrior life?

And where do you begin? What are the things that refresh and energize you? What song, no matter how many times you listen to it, starts your foot tapping? Let us capture that emotion and surround yourself with that feeling.

These are the things that that you need to make part of your present, everyday life. This concept is an approach that focuses on you as a whole person. Get to know yourself and what works for you. Empower your inner Warrior to take charge of your health and your well- being. You are more than your service rifle number, your MOS, your rank, your injuries, or your illnesses. Allow yourself to think about your health, your personal goals, putting yourself first and become your fullest well-being.

Are you thriving? Focus on what you are doing well and what are your challenges. Visualize what you want, what is your purpose. Then write down one SMART goal. Goals are important to your self-care that allows a sense of connection, meaning and purpose. SMART goals are Specific, Measurable, Achievable, Realistic, and Timely. Keep your goals focused and brief.

Making changes in one area in your life can improve your health. If working on a healthier diet, you can lose weight, maybe increase your ability and duration of exercise. These changes can improve your blood pressure, lower your blood sugars, increase your energy during the day and improve your sleep at night. Your overall improvement in your health can free your mind to allow you to focus on improved personal growth and development and improve your relationships with family, friends, and coworkers.

Thinking

Kim Levings
Trainer

Create a strategy to think healthy and properly.

I have been a thinking coach for more than 25 years and know that our ability to think well or not is at the root of almost all outcomes in our lives, both physical and emotional. The "check engine" lights—the physical symptoms and accompanying emotions—are always an indication of dis-ease within our minds. When we ignore those signals, it's just as bad as putting some tape over the real check engine light in your vehicle.

The problem is that thinking well is not something that comes naturally. Our brains store patterns of repeated responses to situations over time. When a response is a negative reaction, triggered with accompanying emotions, it can create "virus code" in our thinking. So, if you have a virus code in your head, how on earth do you get rid of it, or at least replace it with healthy thinking? As my coach likes to say, "You can't see the picture when you're in the frame." Not everyone knows how to find the right help with this, though, and I have come to learn some great tools to help re-code my own thinking and here, pass these ideas on to help others, too.

It begins by a cultivated state of intentional awareness and an attitude of curiosity. Become a great detective as you review your thoughts in any situation. When you experience the physical symptoms that indicate an emotionally charged reaction, give yourself a quick "freeze frame" and ask yourself, "What's really going on here?" That simple action can immediately change the course of the brain. You have shifted it from autopilot, into a conscious state of awareness. If this sounds crazy, think about the last time you drove off somewhere and then couldn't remember if you closed the garage door. Your brain stores automatic patterns so that it doesn't have to actively process and consciously consider everything that you experience. (As a psychiatrist friend said to me, "The brain is basically lazy.")

When you ask yourself that critical question, it fires up your frontal cortex, which takes back the control of thoughts from the limbic part of your brain. Your limbic nervous system is closely aligned with the instinctive, animalistic, and reactive thinking. It is the part of your brain that is designed to protect you from harm, and it keeps you safe. But it also can get the code messed up. The reactive you—the one who slams the door, or yells, or wants to argue—is that automatic part of self. Your reactive self also resides in self-deprecation, depression, victimhood, complaining, blaming...you get the picture!

Now that you've shifted your thinking, what else can you think about in that moment? (Keep in mind that the average speed of a signal along your neural pathways is 268 mph.) Just a couple of seconds is all you need to re-route a thinking pattern in your head. My standard follow up question to the first one is, "What do I really care about here?" Some other questions may include: Will this impact me negatively later? What is making me feel this way right now? Is this situation worth my reaction? What will happen if I choose this reaction? What is another way to handle this? Do I love this person? Do I care about them more than the problem? And so on. You know your mind best—craft your own set of questions to help shift your brain off a path of reactivity.

It is also helpful to breathe for these few seconds. Before you respond, take a deep breath, ask the questions of yourself, and as you let the air back out, the correct response will present itself. Do this often enough, and it becomes less of a concern. Your brain is also more likely to store a new, healthy, pattern when it results in positive, happy emotions. The dopamine and serotonin released in the brain are result of those positive and happy emotions and they are the hormones that help reinforce the storage of a new pattern. To simplify—the brain will do more of what makes it happy.

The next and final step is to plan for a future response. It is possible and essential to re-map your thought patterns. Shifting your thinking from a reactive, pre-programmed path is possible and if you're committed to making the shift, you will. Take the time to write out statements of truth and desire for what you really want—which is often the opposite of how you normally react. These statements should always be in words that you find believable, and they should cause you to experience positive, hopeful emotions when you read them.

Saying these new thoughts out aloud, or writing them out by hand, several times a day will teach your map a new code. This spaced repetition and full involvement of your brain is the required brain training to permanently shift to healthy thinking. Do it often enough and the new thought pattern will take root. Especially in the heat of a trigger moment (when that person lights up your phone, or your partner uses that tone of voice with you, for example), knowing your program code to re-direct your brain in that exact moment will move you quickly to the healthy thinking pattern you want in your life.

I'm so impressed with the basic training our military and first responders undertake as they start out. (Also, that of flight attendants, pilots, emergency room personnel, crisis counselors, and anyone who may be faced with an emergency and/or crisis.) The ability, for example, to gear up and be ready in a matter of seconds comes with repeated, ingrained training. This repetitive and rigorous training teaches the brain (and body) an established pattern of response that becomes so automatic it happens in an instant without engaging the thinking brain.

For the regular folk like myself, it's not often we get this level of pre-programing. They say you never know how you will respond in an emergency until it happens. You can read the notes, listen to whatever safety training is provided, and even practices, but what will you do if that terrible situation occurs? You won't know because it's perhaps not as programed and enforced as the training mentioned above. My advice is that if something is of critical importance and could be a life-or-death scenario, it's probably good for you to engage in your own training and do it often enough that it's an automatic, stored behavior. The bottom line is that we have the power to train and re-train, and un-train our brains.

Accepting that you are at the mercy of your automatic responses is an excuse and a cop out. If you are tolerating bad thinking, chances are you are also suffering from the physical symptoms that will always show up in response to repeated release of cortisol and adrenalin- the stress hormones. To take back full responsibility for your life, you start by taking back the control of your thinking. Stop, breathe, think—life will get better in a second.

Annual Physicals

Michael A. "Bing" Crosby
TOPGUN, United States Navy, United
States Naval Academy

Make it a regular habit to receive your annual physicals and make sure it becomes a part of your newly designed lifestyle.

Annual physicals have been a part of my "Warrior Routine" that commenced in flight school in 1984 and have continued to this day. It was a requirement if you wanted to strap on a jet and fly, so you had no choice back then. But as I grew older, it was clear the benefit of having a productive relationship with those that are trained to provide your medical care was important. It is my belief that "Your health is your responsibility"; you cannot expect others to simply be charged with your care.

The need for constant exercise has been forgotten by most of our society, hence the rise in obesity, cardiac issues, and cancer. For many years, the demands of work seemed to get in the way of a simple walk or 30 minutes of weightlifting but as we grow older, it is even more important.

Warrior Wellness

Dr. Kaylee Koob, Doctor of Occupational Therapy

Warrior Wellness is a prioritization of oneself for self-care, as well as a consideration of the "whole" person.

The profession of occupational therapy can be traced back one-hundred years ago in caring for Veterans after discharge from activity duty. Formally the profession began with an emphasis on arts and crafts as well as leisure activities to assist in occupying the minds of soldiers. However, during World War II, the focus shifted from theories based on leisure and began to include and emphasize science-based rehabilitation models.

Reintegration into civilian life can be extremely challenging, so what do I do as an occupational therapist to address this? As a Doctor of Occupational Therapy, I play a valuable role in addressing the physical, mental, and emotional needs of a soldier's post deployment. I consider the whole person. I consider their individual goals, abilities, and limitations.

It is important to note that post deployment varies in each individual Veteran; the experiences of these soldiers can and are interpreted and internalized differently. Through prioritization of self-care, a Veteran could improve overall energy levels, immunities, and positivity all while lowering the risk of increased stress, depression, anxiety, and other emotional health concerns.

I've learned through my years working with the VA Healthcare System that the best support I can be to a Veteran is to provide compassionate and empathetic listening. However, are there areas of occupational therapy that can contribute to improvements in self-care? Absolutely!

According to a meta-analysis, on average Veterans post-deployment experiencing symptoms of PTSD get on average 5.6 hours of sleep per night; compared to the general population who on average get 6.7 hours of sleep (Khawaja, et al, 2013). This means that 18.4 hours are available to us for self-care out of a twenty-four-hour day.

The first thing you need to do is to make the choice. One needs to choose to take time to prioritize themselves. Choose to engage in something that makes you happy, something that makes you feel better or something to help you relax. Make the task purposeful to you. If you are experiencing hand pain as the result of an injury related or unrelated to your service, paraffin wax treatments may be considered. Not only can it help ease the pain being experienced but the heat of the hands can help one to relax. Also- as your hands will be wrapped up for ten to twenty minutes, you will be unable to participate in much else, thus forcing you to sit back and take time to yourself.

While taking this time I often encourage the Veteran's I work with to practice mindful breathing and active relaxation. Sitting back in your favorite chair, putting your feet up and closing your eyes will allow you to focus in on yourself. Maybe you do this first thing in the morning, then while relaxing you can visualize your goals for the day and how you intend to accomplish them—active relaxation. Maybe you sit back at the end of your day and spend time reflecting on all you accomplished during the day, the week and even your life.

Find your strength and find your purpose. Find ways to take care of yourself that work for you. I believe in the purpose of every Veteran I meet. I believe that not only should they engage in self-care but that they deserve it! The strength, courage and sacrifices have earned this.

Conclusion

"Learn to love the hate. Embrace it. Enjoy it. You earned it. Every-
one is entitled to their own opinion and everyone should have one
about you. Haters are a good problem to have. Nobody hates the
good ones. They hate the great ones."
—KOBE BRYANT

N THE EARLY stages, when we were compiling the contacts
for this book, the two of us exchanged hundreds of emails, text
messages, phone calls, etc. The more we spoke, the more we
started to uncover the far-reaching implications of the content
we were about to share. Having both worked in the Veteran's
Health Administration, providing a lifelong service to the military
community, it was becoming apparent that this was our central
topic of discussion, and it had been ruminating as a narrative
for everything we were doing inside and outside of work. This
continued exploration, curation, and writing came about on the
success of our previous book *The Warrior's Book of Virtues.*

As we canvassed for contributors, we found men and women
doing remarkable things for their self-compassion, wellbeing, and
mind-body connection. This stirred great emotions within us and
made us realize that we can be doing a whole lot more for our
own personal wellness. The more conversations we had with the
valorous contributors showcased within these pages, the more we
realized there are so many layers to the suffering and trauma for
those fellow WARRIORS who are not so lucky.

Semper Fidelis,
Nick Benas, USMC & Buzz Bryan, USN

Afterword

by Sarah Plummer Taylor, MSW

FROM MEDITATION TO marksmanship and bubble baths to basketball, research and anecdotes, guidance from subject matter experts and laypeople, the authors of this book have covered the spectrum of resilience advice. In reading this compilation of works by my fellow veterans, I loved seeing that, in one way or another, they've all authentically elucidated the three empirically-validated pillars of resilience: self-care, social support, and spiritual practices. There are, of course, many different forms of practice within each category, meaning there's room to personalize and customize what works for you based on your personality, resources, and interest. Moreover, there are many places where the key pillars overlap with one another. For instance, social support and spiritual practices often overlap when we are doing service work in the community with members of our place of worship.

But when life gets complicated, simplifying is often incredibly helpful, and having been in the trenches myself, I know that simplicity has been empowering in my most difficult times. I loved serving in the military, *and* it was a time full of intense challenges and choices. In a beautiful variety of ways, this book lays out some options for *choices* to make about our personal wellness path, and that's what I so appreciate about it.

Thus, my encouragement to you would be *"simplify to amplify."* At first, choose just one or two things from this book to either re-engage in or start anew. Keep in mind that although there is a military veteran focus in *The Resilient Warrior*, wellness and resilience is relevant for us *all* and transitions are pretty universally some of the trickiest times in our lives. In their journey from military life to civilian life, veterans can experience a loss of identity, loss of community, and loss of a sense of purpose. That space between point A and point B is often a scary one for most of us, a kind of a space where we're swinging between trapezes, having just let go of one without having yet grabbed the other. Even when transition is something we see as a positive change, change is still change, and change is hard for most of us. Couple with a worldwide pandemic and competing priorities, and we can all become vulnerable to burn out. We need something more than "self-care isn't selfish" sayings to help you stay the course.

Certainly, you have already cultivated resilience in some regard through your experiences in the military and beyond. My hope is that this book offered you a reminder (or some new ideas) for how to navigate these stressful times and keep doing the work you feel called to do—all while living the life you deem most valuable efficiently and effectively.

Now more than ever in these unusual times, we need to be creative as veterans as we find ourselves in a community or at a workplace where we may be one of only a few who have served in the military, or in a new home where we may feel disconnected. Resilience will help us bridge the gap as we enhance our understanding of how important connection—to self and with others—is so we strive even more to make it happen in whatever ways we can, and we become better able to think more clearly such that we feel fresh and available to our work and our families.

There's this old saying that if the only tool you have is a hammer, everything looks like a nail. The "just keep going" tool isn't enough. You can make it through life that way, sure, but you're not going to feel anywhere near your best, be your best with your friends and family, perform your best at work. We simply *have* to figure out new ways to connect to our sense of *self*, connect with *others*, and connect with our sense of *purpose*. So today, and beyond, I encourage you to spend some time building out your toolkit so you have a range of responses at your disposal, so you have more tools in your toolkit.

Again, simplify to amplify—just pick one or two things to focus on changing. If you try to change a dozen things, you'll likely reinforce the misbelief that "nothing works." Explore mindfulness apps or online classes, reach out to a friend who you know is into this stuff, spend more time reading additional books about resilience than scrolling social media, or simply intuitively guide yourself. Mindfulness and resilience-building is *exactly* about increasing our range of responses, bulletproofing our psyche, and building our skillsets. Resilience is not about having one perfect plan to handle single every situation; it's about being adaptive, responsive, able to pivot, empowering you to be flexible, dynamic and creative.

Veterans: we are *assets*, so let's take care of ourselves like we really believe that, and bring our strength fully into the world. I want to live in a world with more resilient veterans. Don't you?! So, please, I *urge* you, choose to take care of yourself enough such that you are able to bring your gifts forward. Because, the truth is, we've all faced battles…in combat, or divorce, illness, loss, violence, sorrows, and setbacks. But we are resilient. We have choice. And from choice, hope.

Ask yourself, where do you grow stronger, one *choice* at a time?

We served, we will continue to serve, and we are the change we seek. We can do this!

I sincerely wish you the very best along your resilience journey and am grateful to have been a part of it in any way at all. Warmly,

—Sarah Plummer Taylor, MSW

Resources

Clarity Child Guidance Center

Clarity Child Guidance Center is the only nonprofit in South Texas providing a continuum of mental health care for children, ages 3 to 17, and their families. Clarity CGC treats children and adolescents who are experiencing a range of emotional, mental, and behavioral illnesses from ADHD and anxiety to suicidal ideation, bipolar disorder and/or schizophrenia. In 2019, it provided services for 9,145 children and their families.

Military families overcome challenges that most civilian families cannot imagine. Over time, these unique stressors can take a toll on even the most resilient kids. Unfortunately, due to frequent transitions, it is easy to miss warning signs that a child needs help. Whether you are active duty, reserve, National Guard, or a veteran, Clarity Child Guidance Center dedicates 13 military-specific pages of its website (claritycgc.org/military) with guidance on steps to prepare your kids for the obstacles and common challenges of military life and how to respond to children's mental health struggles. To educate clinicians and other credentialed professionals who work closely with military children, CCGC also offers Claritycon—an intensive training regarding children's mental health--with a minimum of two CEUs focused on helping military families.

Nathan John

www.nathan-john.com

Facebook: www.facebook.com/decisionpointbook

Instagram: www.instagram.com/nj_author/

Twitter: https://twitter.com/nj_author

LinkedIn: www.linkedin.com/in/nathan-j-davis/

Devoted to a Soldier (www.devotedtoasoldier.com)

Oscar Mike Radio (www.oscarmikeradio.com)

Rev. Bernice Sykes, Ph.D. "Doc Bunny"

19SeventySixCoaching www.19SeventySixCoaching.com

Email: docbunny2020@gmail.com

Twitter: @docbunny2020

Instagram: docbunny2020

Colleen Canestrari

Instagram: @Collbarefoot, @Wyattthewonderpup, @TheRustedPumpkin

WordPress: www.therustedpumpkin.wordpress.com/

MSgt Brice R Snyder

brice.snyder.8412@gmail.com

Instagram: @soapboxsnyder, @live2serve2live

Monique Medved

Website: www.moniquemedved.com.au

Instagram: @moniquemedved

YouTube: www.youtube.com/channel/
UCp7zZOZcANBqKYigPz6c7zw

Charissa Schmidt

You can find Charissa online at www.windhorseonline.word-press.com and on Facebook as Charissa Schmidt, Windhorse Farm and Sisu Counseling Services.

Yasenka Counseling & Coaching, LLC.

www.yasenkacounseling.com/

(603) 235-3499

Dani Rocco

www.danirocco.com

www.devotedtoasoldier.com

Facebook: www.facebook.com/danielle.datilio.rocco, www.facebook.com/Danielle.rooco.1

LinkedIn: www.linkedin.com/in/danielle-rocco-606b933

Instagram: www.instagram.com/danielle.rocco.1

Gwen Lawrence

www.gwenlawrence.com

Twitter: @gwenlawrence

Instagram: @gwenlawrence

Facebook: Gwen Lawrence

STEPHEN SUCHY

New England Ninjutsu, Wallingford, CT

http://www.newenglandninjutsu.com/

(203) 303-4893

KATE DEEKS

www.katedeeks.com

@reallytalltruth, @OMNES

Coaching, healing, and creative services available

HOPE FOR THE DAY PROJECT RED

www.hftd.org/red-team

Facebook: www.facebook.com/groups/projectredteam

SARAH PLUMMER TAYLOR, MSW

www.SemperSarah.com

Warrior Contributors

HEATHER CLARK

A US Navy Combat Veteran, Heather Clark served as an intelligence analyst for Navy Intelligence and Special Operations. Heather holds a B.S. in Psychology, minor in Evolutionary Anthropology and is a graduate student in Public Health at Purdue University. After leaving the military, Heather experienced a great sense of loss and purpose. She also struggled with her own mental health challenges from service. She returned to the ancient practice of yoga with the SEAL teams she served with in Afghanistan. As Heather returned to her own practice, she also saw a need in the veteran community for more holistic options for recovery. The gaps she saw in current public health care programs were that they were designed for the public, not the military. She then started her journey to research these gaps and find a way to design a holistic program that used a soldier mindset. A mindset that used VETSPEAK, a method that uses the terminology, movement, and the culture of the military. A program that integrated in dry fire positions, marching commands and yoga exercises that had been taught since basic training. She then took her knowledge of this ancient practice and combined it with her academic knowledge in Psychology and Public Health and her own personal experiences in cognitive behavior and exposure therapy treatments to create a unique military style yoga program.

COLLEEN CANESTRARI

Instagram: @Collbarefoot, @Wyattthewonderpup,
@TheRustedPumpkin

WordPress: www.therustedpumpkin.wordpress.com/

DR. JOSH ESSERY

Dr. Josh Essery, Director of Outpatient Clinical Services at Clarity Child Guidance Center, provides outpatient family, group, and individual psychotherapy as well as psychological assessment services. He is also involved in the supervision and training of psychology residents. He is Board Certified in Clinical Psychology by the American Board of Professional Psychology. A Clinical Professor in the Psychiatry Department at the University of Texas Health Science Center at San Antonio, Dr. Essery is a member of Division 39 of the American Psychological Association, the American Group Psychotherapy Association, the San Antonio Group Psychotherapy Association and the San Antonio Society for Psychoanalytic Studies.

NATHAN JOHN

Nathan John, a British Army Veteran, Nathan joined the Royal Signals in 1997. Completing tours in Kosovo and Sierra Leone, Nathan subsequently commissioned from the ranks (enlisted service) into the Officer Corps in 2006. Twelve years later and two further tours of Iraq and Afghanistan, Nathan left the Army after 20 years to pursue a career in business. He has a growing personal property portfolio and has taken up the position as the Chief of Staff in a Private Family Office. Growing the family's business interests and leading an international staff, he is now a director in no less than 5 of the business entities. Nathan has used his position to recruit ex-military personnel into the business group and has also negotiated preferential terms for veterans in starting their own fitness franchise.

Ashton Cantou

Ashton Cantou is a Certified Transformational Life Coach and Leadership Coach for High Performance. She has survived her inner battles with substance abuse, self-sabotage, depression, and anxiety. As an educational leader, she has held hundreds of workshops, masterclasses, and one-on-one training sessions over the last decade. With her immense wisdom and expertise, Ashton has proven to be successful in helping numerous people including veterans heal trauma and create both success and fulfillment in their lives.

Michael "Bing" Crosby

Michael "Bing" Crosby is a 1983 graduate of the United States Naval Academy and earned a Master of Science from the University of Southern California in Los Angeles in 1991. He is also a graduate of the US Navy Fighter Weapons School "TOPGUN" and Allied Air Forces Central Europe "Tactical Leadership Program" in Jever, Germany. Mr. Crosby has logged over 3,000 hours in multiple tactical jet aircraft, including, the F-14, F/A-18, B-1B, Mirage 2000, Tornado GR1, Harrier, and the F-16N.

CDR Crosby was diagnosed in 2015 with Prostate Cancer at the Phoenix VA but chose a course of treatment outside the VA. In 2016, because of the diagnosis of prostate cancer and finding out firsthand the lack of education or awareness around the disease in the VA, CDR Crosby founded Veterans Prostate Cancer Awareness Inc., a 501c3 nonprofit focused on providing educational resources to Veterans and Active-Duty Military. Since discovering his own prostate cancer and learning that prostate is the number one cancer diagnosis in the VA it has become clear that Veterans and men in general are not paying attention to this disease. The simple mission of raising awareness has led to a partnership with ZERO-The End of Prostate Cancer and a growing awareness within the VA of the need to educate all men of the importance of annual screening for prostate cancer. If found early, it has a 99 percent chance of cure but if left at a later stage those chances reduce to less than 30 percent.

CORIN CUNNINGHAM

Corin Cunningham has worked in healthcare management for over 10 years, both in the non-profit and private sector. She has an educational background in Anthropology and Public Health and training in Practice and Operations Management, Positive Leadership, Customer Service, meditation, and Reiki. A caregiver at heart, Corin has learned the importance of taking care of oneself first and foremost so that one can, in doing so, take care of others.

KATE DEEKS

www.katedeeks.com

@reallytalltruth @OMNES

R. A. FARRER, USMC, B.A., M.B.A.

Irreverent Warriors District Commander, Department of Tennessee

www.irreverentwarriors.com

Cell: (615) 490-5715

Irreverent Warriors

(501c3) Tax ID 47-4789126

CAROL GEE, M.A.

Carol Gee, M.A, served nearly eight years on active duty. With an active-duty spouse (long retired) and wanting to continue to play a role in the military, she joined the Air Force Reserves, serving 14 years before retiring as a Technical Sergeant, E-6). Nine years ago, she retired again after 28 years in higher education at the university level, to become a published author and freelance writer, www.VenusChronicles.net. She and her spouse of 47 years live in an Atlanta suburb.

JOE HAMILTON AND BEN KING

Joe Hamilton and Ben King are both Army veterans. Between the two of them is over 50 months of combat deployments to both Iraq and Afghanistan, and 4 Purple Hearts. United by their shared sense of continuing service to both the Veteran Community and the United States Military they combined their expertise in both Mindfulness and Marksmanship to create the Armor Down Mindful Marksmanship program.

Joe Hamilton currently leads a DOD team focused on cutting edge research related to shooting and use-of-force for the US Military. He is also a DOD/DOJ certified firearms/tactical instructor as well as a Master Class competitive shooter in multiple disciplines. Ben King is a certified mindfulness instructor who has taught hundreds of veterans how to armor down with mindfulness. His work honoring fallen warriors and teaching veterans mindfulness has been featured by WTOP radio, The Washington Post and on NBC. Ben is a contributing author to numerous books and publications including *Bullet Proofing the Psyche: Preventing Mental Health Problems in our Military and Veterans*. Ben was honored in 2016 by National Geographic in "Veterans Voices; Remarkable Stories of Heroism, Sacrifice and Honor" featuring vets from WWII to the present.

KATE HENDRICKS THOMAS, PHD

Kate Hendricks Thomas, PhD is a behavioral medicine researcher and Master Certified Health Education Specialist. She studies evidence-based mental fitness and peak performance and is the author of several books. Kate is passionate about education and teaches for George Mason University's Department of Global and Community Health. Her TEDx speeches provide a glimpse into Dr. Kate's unique ability to make science accessible and actionable for everyday audiences. Dr. Kate's background as an academic researcher, storyteller, and U.S. Marine Corps veteran positions her to communicate credibly to a variety of audiences. She is a writer and researcher at heart and has authored over 100 scientific publications and presentations. Her behavioral health research, published in journals like Best Practices in Mental Health, the Journal of Environmental Psychology, and Military Behavioral Health, has been praised as "masterful" and "constructive." She writes for a diverse array of popular blogs and newspapers—her social commentary has been featured on NPR and BBC and published in The Hill and in The Washington Post.

Dr. Kaylee Koob, OTD, OTR/L

Doctor of Occupational Therapy

Sioux Falls VA Medical Center

Lieutenant Colonel Ross "RAW" Hobbs

Lieutenant Colonel Ross "RAW" Hobbs is a graduate of the US Air Force Academy with over 2000 flight hours, and is currently the Chief of Weapons and Tactics at US Air Forces Central Command at Shaw AFB, SC. He has deployed several times to multiple locations throughout the world, including the Middle East where he accumulated nearly 500 hours of combat time. He is the living embodiment of leadership, health, and strength.

Amanda Hudes

As the creator of Smiling Through Chaos LLC, Amanda dedicates her time to helping women and couples smile more, stress less, and look and feel their best during their event planning experience through Event Planning and Wellness Coaching. From high profile clientele to the neighbor next door, Amanda appreciates every single client, creating one-of-a-kind, amazing events and moments for each. It's extremely important to Amanda that she understands her clients, so she puts tremendous emphasis into forming relationships and getting to know their likes, dislikes, style, and what is really important to them. Amanda is the author of Amazon bestseller *Smiling Through The Chaos of Wedding Planning*, a guide to helping people smile through the process of planning their big day.

TARA HUNTER, RN

Tara is a devoted advocate for veterans in her community, family and loved ones, helping them get available resources and engaging them in positive lifestyle modifications with the goal of attaining a fulfilling-happy life.

VANESSA JACOBY, PhD, ABPP

Vanessa serves as an advisor with Clarity Child Guidance Center and one of the editors of its information campaigns for military families. She is a Licensed Clinical Psychologist with a child specialization and is Board Certified in Cognitive and Behavioral Psychology. She is an Assistant Professor in the Division of Behavioral Medicine at the University of Texas Health Science Center and a member of the STRONG STAR Multidisciplinary Research Consortium and the Consortium to Alleviate PTSD, whose mission is to alleviate and prevent posttraumatic stress disorder (PTSD) and other deployment related problems in active duty service members and their families. In her work at STRONG STAR, Dr. Jacoby conducts prevention and supportive programs with military families with young children experiencing deployment.

Gwen Lawrence, BS LMT E-RYT500

Gwen Lawrence is an Experienced Registered Yoga Teacher (E-RYT 500) with Yoga Alliance, which acknowledges the completion of a yoga teacher training with an approved and active Registered Yoga School (RYS). Gwen has been a practicing fitness professional since 1990. Her current practice includes private yoga training, class instruction, team instruction and her Power Yoga for Sports, sports specific training, International travel to teach, TV appearances, Writing, Workshops and radio contributions. You can become a certified Yoga Coach through her online training, like people around the world in 18 countries are taking advantage of. Gwen's unique combination of dance, massage therapy, and yoga training experience, coupled with her extensive knowledge of anatomy and nutrition, provides her clients and athletes with overwhelming results.

Monique Medved

Website: www.moniquemedved.com.au

Instagram: @moniquemedved

YouTube: www.youtube.com/channel/
   UCp7zZOZcANBqKYigPz6c7zw

Dani Rocco

Dani Rocco is a mother, wife and lifelong entrepreneur. Growing up as a professional ballerina developed her commitment and dedication to everything that life has to offer. As an adult, her athletic skills assisted her in becoming a successful business owner. At the age of 18, she started working for her family's gymnastics school and took the company from bankruptcy to financial abundance. The school maxed out its student capacity very quickly. After 23 years of being the CEO, Dani left her family business to follow her passion of being a life coach and relationship expert. Becoming a Marine mom changed her life and she soon realized her heart and mission was in serving our military and veterans. She is now author of *Devoted to a Soldier* and co-author with Les Brown of *Own Your Dreams* and *1 Habit*.

CHARISSA SCHMIDT

Charissa Schmidt is a licensed professional counselor practicing in Oregon state. She comes from a career military family and has family members who have served in every major conflict since the American Revolution. She is the first generation not to enlist, instead she chose to serve civilians in the mental health field. She currently practices and teaches traditional cavalry horsemanship.

RYAN SHANNON

Ryan Shannon served just under nine years in the submarine force with the United States Navy, before being medically retired due to injuries sustained (physical and mental) while serving on active duty. After his retirement, he returned to school where he completed his bachelor's degree and also received his MBA with a focus on Organizational Leadership. He is currently the Director of Project R.E.D. Team with a non-profit organization called Hope for the Day where they focus on proactive suicide prevention and mental health education. He is also a training instructor for Siemens where he serves as co-chair for the company's North American Veterans ERG.

JAMES SMITH

James Smith was born in Ft. Worth, Texas and entered the Army shortly after graduating High School. Upon completion of Basic Combat Training and Advanced Individual Training, he was assigned to C/10 MLRS Ft. Carson, CO where he served as a radio operator. Smith attended Special Forces Assessment and Selection in 1999 and graduated the Special Forces Qualification

Course in 2000, after which he was assigned to Bravo Company, 1st Battalion, 5th Special Forces Group (Airborne) where he remained for just over a decade.

His successful career has included seven deployments to Iraq and Afghanistan as well as several other countries located in Southwest Asia. He is now a blog writer, aspiring author, and an entrepreneur whose mission is to empower other veterans by sharing his story and lessons learned to assist the veteran community to rediscover themselves and their purpose.

MASTER SERGEANT BRICE "SOAPBOX" SNYDER

June 2, 1999: Enlisted into the Marine Corps on Parris Island, SC

2000–2003: 0311 Light Armored Reconnaissance Crewman and Scout with several 4th and 3rd LAR Units

2003–2005: Operation Iraqi Freedom

22005–2007: 0311 Infantry Training Instructor and Enhanced Marksmanship Instructor, Platoon Sgt I&I 1/25th Marines

2007–2010: 8411 Recruiting Duty 1st Marine Corps District

2010–present: 8412 Career Recruiter 1St Marine Corps District

HEIKE SOMMER

Heike Sommer is a Psychiatric Mental Health Nurse Practitioner who had the honor to do a 1-year long internship for clinical hours at the VA in Portland, OR. Working with veterans on PTSD related issues gave her a lot of respect for the men and women who served this beautiful country and paid with a high price of mental health issues to be our often-underappreciated heroes. She still works with some veterans in her community mental health as well in her private practice. Born and raised in Germany with both grandfathers having served in wars and parents who grew up in the midst of WWII, she has had a first-hand experience of PTSD and how unprocessed trauma can affect daily life and sleep.

STEPHEN SUCHY

Stephen Suchy joined the US Marines on October 28, 1975, and served three years active duty; he also spent four years in the reserves while finishing college. In 1982, he became a police officer and worked as a patrolman until 2009. As a dedicated first responder for his whole career, he also served as a SWAT officer for 24 of his 28 years of service. In 2009, Suchy retired from the department and became a state investigator for the public defender's office, serving his first 10 years in a major CT city. He was promoted to an investigator with the CT Innocence Project, a sub-unit of the public defender's office that investigates cases of those serving life in prison for murder.

REV. BERNICE SYKES, PH.D.

"Doc Bunny" is a Holistic Life Coach specializing in Spiritual Leadership, Restorative Justice, creating Healthy Workspaces, and Reputation Management. She also is a School Choice Advocate who creates homeschool curriculum. Her "hard love" approach to problem solving and commitment to results stems from service in the U.S. Army. She is the Founder and CEO of 19SeventySixCoaching. Doc Bunny is an award-winning and nationally recognized veteran and mental health advocate who specializes in Suicide Prevention and Mental Health Awareness. She believes people have the ability to transform at the deepest level when identifying their ability to love yourself through the toughest situations. Doc Bunny was raised and lives in Las Vegas, Nevada and loves to travel at any opportunity. She has been featured in Learning Success.

JOE WADANOLI

Joe Wadanoli, a Master Barber. is the owner of and Barber at Joe and Co. Barbershop in Madison, Connecticut. Specializing in military haircuts, Joe works closely with many veterans, active-duty military, first responder and front-line workers. Although Joe was not fit for active duty, he did volunteer for five years in the United States Coast Guard Auxiliary, where he aided local mariners and his local community in auxiliary and joint Coast Guard operations and promoted safe waterways. A self-proclaimed artist and is a versed guitar player, Joe lives in his hometown with his wife Charlene and his bulldogs Buzz and Bailey.

RICH WALTON "BOX AND ONE" BASKETBALL

Rich Walton specializes in teaching basketball skill development and is the founder of Skill Development Coach.

HERBERT D. WELTE, JR

Herbert D. Welte, Jr (Bud) is a retired farmer living in North Dakota. He taught industrial arts at the high school and college level in Connecticut for 15 years before moving to North Dakota in 1969 with his wife and two children to take over the family farm. He was drafted by the U.S. Army in 1956 and served two years with the 534th Field Artillery Battalion, in Bad Kissingen, Germany.

KORTNEY YASENKA

Owner of YCC, Kortney is a licensed clinical mental health counselor who provides individual, family, and group therapy, as well as life coaching to children, adolescents, adults, parents, and families. Kortney is certified in trauma focused cognitive behavioral therapy and has experience working with veterans and active military personnel. With over 15 years of experience, Kortney has experience working in community mental health, school systems, and private practice while specializing in mood disorders, school and work-related issues, life transitions, and self-esteem.

Bibliography

Drive Wines. (2020, November 18). Retrieved December 20, 2020, from https://www.drivewines.com/

Fannin, J. (2020). Dr. Jeffrey Fannin. (H. C. Clark, Interviewer)

Farrer, A. (2021). The Silkies Hike. Retrieved January 16, 2021, from https://www.irreverentwarriors.com/

Galotti, K. M. (2014). Cognitive Psychology. Thousand Oaks: Sage.

Garcia, J. (2019). Former Secretary of the VA. (H. C. Clark, Interviewer)

Khawaja, Imran S et al. "Nocturnal Awakening & Sleep Duration in Veterans with PTSD: An Actigraphic Study." Pakistan journal of medical sciences vol. 29,4 (2013): 991-6. doi:10.12669/pjms.294.3831

Lee, D. (1976). *Tai chi chuan: The philosophy of yin and yang and its application*. Burbank, CA: Ohara Publications.

Ralph Lewis, M. (021). What exactly is a thought and information physical? Retrieved from Psychology Today: https://www.psychology-today.com/us/blog/finding-purpose/201902/what-actually-is-thought-and-how-is-information-physical

Tiwari, M. (1995). A Life of Balance, The Complete Guide to Ayurvedic Nutrition & Body Types. Rochester: Healing Arts Press.

US Navy. (2020). US Navy Regulations. Retrieved from US Navy PRT Regulations: www.mynavyhr.navy.mil

Yogafit. (2020). Yoga for Veterans with PTSD. Yogafit.

About the Authors

Nick Benas grew up in Guilford, Connecticut. The author of *Mental Health Emergencies*, *Warrior Wisdom*, *Tactical Mobility*, and co-author of *The Warrior's Book of Virtues*, Benas is a former United States Marine Sergeant and Iraqi Combat Veteran with a background in Martial Arts (2nd Dan Black Belt in Tae Kwon-Do and Green Belt Instructor in Marine Corps Martial Arts Program). Nick attended Southern Connecticut State University for his undergraduate degree in Sociology and his M.S. in Public Policy. He has been featured for his business success and entrepreneurship by more than 50 major media outlets, including Entrepreneur Magazine, Men's Health, ABC, FOX, ESPN, and CNBC.

Richard "Buzz" Bryan is currently the Outreach Coordinator for the West Palm Beach VA medical center. The co-author of *The Warrior's Book of Virtues,* Buzz previously served as the OEF/OIF Transition Patient Advocate (TPA) for the Veterans Integrated Service Network (VISN4) based in Pittsburgh, PA for ten years, working specifically with Iraq & Afghanistan veterans. Buzz was a member of the Navy/Marine Corps team and retired from the United States Navy in July 2011 after 22 years of honorable service as a Fleet Marine Force Senior Chief Hospital Corpsman.